FENG SHUI

MARKED FOR DEATH

FENG SHUI
ADVENTURES
BY
BRUCE A. BAUGH
CHRIS PRAMAS
GREG STOLZE
JOHN TYNES
AND
ALLEN VARNEY

Dædalus Entertainment, Inc.

DAEDALUS ENTERTAINMENT, INC. PRESENTS

MARKED FOR DEATH

FIVE CHAPTERS IN THE SECRET WAR

WRITERS
BRUCE A. BAUGH, CHRIS PRAMAS, GREG STOLZE, JOHN TYNES, AND ALLEN VARNEY

ILLUSTRATORS
DAVID FOODEN, HEATHER HUDSON, JON WEIMAN

COVER ARTIST
MARK TEDIN

EXECUTIVE PRODUCERS
JOSE GARCIA AND MARIA GARCIA

EDITOR & DEVELOPER
JOHN TYNES

ART DIRECTOR & GRAPHIC DESIGNER
DANIEL GELON

PLAYTESTERS
JASON ADAMS, JON BJELLAND, BRIAN THE NINJA, TRAVIS BRYANT, TYLER CHILDERS, KEVIN GERL, CHRIS GORILLA, MARCUS GREGORY, SAMUEL HANDELMAN, HARRIET HOYEM, TORE HOYEM, BOB KRAUS, BILL MULLEN, EMMA TROLLMAN, FRANK TROLLMAN, TED TROLLMAN, JASON UTZ, ROB VAUX, ROB WILKINS

SPECIAL THANKS
ROB, JOSE, MARIA, LYNN, IAN, AND JESPER FOR BEING SWELL; CAPTAIN WOW FOR BITING ALL THE RIGHT TOES; THE PAGAN BOYS FOR LETTING ME WORK; DAMON & JENNIFER FOR THE WELL-TIMED VISIT; NICOLE AT ADVENTURES UNLIMITED, STEVE & ANDY AT ARCANE, AND SCOTT AT PYRAMID FOR DIGGING OUR STUFF.

 For questions or comments, write us at the address above. You can also call us at (206) 232-3040, or send email to jgarcia@halcyon.com. Check us out on the world wide web at:
http://www.aracnet.com/~bruce/daedalus/index.html

CONTENTS

1 INT. THE BUN FESTIVAL—EVENING 1

This is a seedy topless nightclub in the Kowloon district of Hong Kong, run by the Triad gangster Fast Eddie Lo. There's a big crowd of surly low-lifes and drunken businessmen. Off to one side, our heroes sit at a table nursing drinks. They are ARCHIE "TWO FISTS" JACKSON, a big bruiser of a guy; TSUI WOO, a magic-wielding cop; DIANA SORENSEN, ex-special forces; and TOMMY CHO, a scrappy kid.

TOMMY
(wide-eyed at the strippers)
This rules!

TWO FISTS
Close your eyes, kid. You ain't ready for this kinda entertainment.

DIANA
Archie, the kid waxed Happy Cheung while you were picking up your teeth. He's entitled.

TWO FISTS
Hey, I was gonna knock that guy's block off! I was just catching my wind.

TOMMY
Ha! I think you were down for the count! Happy kicked your butt up and down Temple Street!

TWO FISTS
If you weren't just a kid I'd—

TSUI
Enough, enough! Two fists, cut the kid some slack. He did good.

TOMMY beams and slurps his soda. TWO FISTS looks sullen. Just then, FAST EDDIE LO comes out of a back room, surrounded by four burly MOOKS. The group heads over to the table.

FAST EDDIE
Well, well. If it isn't my favorite group of low-lifes.

DIANA
How can you tell us apart from your customers?

FAST EDDIE
It's easy. My customers show me face. You people came in here demanding information and flew off the handle when my little brothers tried to teach you respect.

TSUI
Hey, Eddie, come on. That was uncalled for. We took out the Poison Thorns just like we said!

FAST EDDIE
That is true. This is why my men will not kill you now.
(pause)
However, they're still going to teach you a lesson.

The MOOKS crack their knuckles and look mean. FAST EDDIE steps out of the way, smiling.

DIANA stands up fast and kicks the table over, knocking one MOOK back a couple steps while the rest step away. We see she's brought out a pair of nunchakus. TWO FISTS comes out of his chair with an uppercut and sends a MOOK sprawling. TOMMY leaps onto the next table, spilling drinks, and goes into a kung fu stance. TSUI is left sitting in his chair, smoking a cigarette. He blows out a cloud of smoke while everyone else stands and glares. Blue magical energy crackles around his head.

TSUI
Okay. Let's rumble.

MAIN TITLES BEGIN

JOHN TYNES

INTRODUCTION

The status quo, as they say, ain't what it used to be. That's certainly true of the adventures in this book. Unlike many published RPG adventures—where the end of the scenario means that everything is back the way it was—the world of *Feng Shui* is constantly changing, constantly moving forward. The dynamics of the secret war are such that you almost can't help but make an enemy every time you walk out your front door. In *Marked For Death,* your unwitting players can get on the bad side of Triad gangsters, the Architects of the Flesh, the Jammers, the Four Monarchs, the Eaters of the Lotus and the Ascended. (Yeah, sounds like the gang's all here.) If they're smart, they'll make some friends in the Guiding Hand during the last scenario—but everyone else in the secret war is going to cross the PCs off their Christmas list. Like I said, that's the nature of *Feng Shui*—there's a war on, with many factions involved, and for every action your players take, someone else will take an equal and opposite reaction. It won't take long for the PCs to all be *Marked For Death.*

You can use these adventures in any order, and ignore some if you like. I've arranged them in the book in a fairly natural progression from simple to complex.

"Brinks!" is where we begin. This little doozie will seem pretty straightforward to your players, as they foil a bank robbery and beat up on a bunch of Triad mooks. The adventure will be over before you know it—but behind the scenes, the PCs are in big trouble. They'll have hacked off the Architects of the Flesh, not to mention the Triads, and both groups are ready and willing to cause trouble in the future at your command.

"Blood for the Master" is next on the hit parade. It's just another night at Rikki Ko's Ultra Fine Pizza, until a bunch of demon cultists, demon hunters, and just plain old demons turn the place into a massive free-for-all. Suitable for beginning characters or for those fresh from "Baptism of Fire" in the rulebook, this is a knock-down, drag-out fight from start to finish.

On your PCs' next trip into the Netherworld, they get approached by a mad scientist out for revenge—or is he? A whirlwind tour of several scenic butt-kickings follows in "Pai Lai," including a little jaunt to 2056 and a look at life under the Buro.

Speaking of the Netherworld, "Pai Lai" is a good place to introduce the plot threads of "The Shape of Guilt." This isn't a stand-alone adventure, but rather a sub-plot for you to work into your campaign. It deals with the Four Monarchs, the IKTV (Inner Kingdom Television) station, Lusignan the Fool, and a whole bunch of Netherworld Rabble. Oh yeah—the ghost of the Monarchs' dead father is around, too. He's on live TV, you see, and he's got a story to tell.

Going out with a bang, "Shaolin Heartbreak" is the longest adventure in the book. A love-struck Guiding Hand monk is on the trail of an innerwalker named Kam Li, who is tracking an ancient sorcerer named Phanom Rung, who is tracking an HK movie star named Maureen Wei-Jing, who is… well, you'll see. "Shaolin Heartbreak" is a real rouser of a tale, with plenty of plot twists and great characters.

There's a lot of good stuff in this book, and I think you'll enjoy it. I'd like to call your attention to the many cool GMCs found throughout, many of whom can survive the adventures to become parts of your campaign. Look for these opportunities and take them, and you'll have a full-fledged campaign up and running before you know it. The geomancer Chu Po in "Shaolin Heartbreak," Rikki Ko and the whole neighborhood of "Blood for the Master," the Triad enforcers of "Brinks!," and others are all ripe for use in further adventures of your own. I've tried to gear this book so that you can't help but end up with a bunch of ongoing plotlines, characters, locations, allies, and enemies. Don't treat any of the GMCs as disposable people that the PCs will never meet again; people have an odd way of popping up again in the secret war, and you never know whose help you'll need tomorrow.

In conclusion, get ready to blow things up and have some serious fun. Now turn the page, and let the adventures begin.

The sedan is moving swiftly through the streets of Hong Kong. Several more identical sedans are nearby, to the sides and behind. In the back seat are DEN SO SUK, LEE HA HO, and MAO KAI LEE; all three are Triad gangsters. LEE HA HO and MAO KAI LEE, both in their mid-twenties, are fiddling with handguns. DEN SO SUK, in his late thirties, is their superior; he sits calmly.

MAO KAI LEE
(admiring his Desert Eagle .357 Magnum)
I'm telling you, you want that Magnum stopping power. If you put a bullet in someone, you want to know that he's going down. I don't care if he bites it with that one shot or not—he's still gonna be in a world of hurt if you pop him one of these.

LEE HA HO
(checking the magazine in his Glock 17)
Bull. You watch too much Dirty Harry.

MAO KAI LEE
Hey, Dirty Harry doesn't carry a Desert Eagle! Give me some credit, eh?

LEE HA HO
(chuckling)
Sure, sure, little brother. But when you're out of bullets, don't get in the way of my Glock. I'll still be bringing them down while you're fumbling for ammo.

MAO KAI LEE
(boastful)
If you're good, you don't need a lotta bullets.

LEE HA HO
If you're good, more bullets means more hits. I don't need that brute force crap. Give me my target, I'll take him down with a frisbee if I have to.

MAO KAI LEE
Hah! Besides, Dirty Harry's old and crusty. Chow Yun-Fat…now there's a man who knows how to use a gun.

LEE HA HO
Yeah, right. He never reloads, man! And two guns at once? I don't think so. He may be cool, but if he's your idol you won't last long in this line of work.

MAO KAI LEE
Longer than you!

DEN SO SUK
Enough! You two and your movies will be the death of me. Now get ready—we'll be at the bank soon. Don't get all excited. Take the guards out, but try not to hurt the customers more than you have to.

MAO KAI LEE
(sighting down the barrel out the window)
Pow! Hah! Someone gives me trouble, they're going down.

DEN SO SUK
Not if you can help it. If someone gives us trouble, we have other ways of dealing with the situation.

DEN SO SUK reaches into a pocket inside his suit coat and pulls out an AGONY GRENADE—a hand-held arcanowave device that looks like a normal (if sleek) grenade with a weird claw on top for a pin. MAO KAI LEE and LEE HA HO look on admiringly as the grenade crackles with visible magical energy. MAO KAI LEE whistles.

DEN SO SUK
And if you two and your brothers don't screw this up, there's a lot more where this came from…

BRUCE A. BAUGH

BRINKS!

ILLUSTRATED BY HEATHER HUDSON

Premise: The PCs are at a bank, doing business or meeting someone. Yawn.
The Twist: The bank is on a good feng shui site, and the Architects of the Flesh have recruited the Triads in a plan to seize control of the site. For starters, how about a bank robbery?
The Climax: It's a John Woo slo-mo killing spree when the PCs hit a Victoria Peak mansion crawling with Triad mooks.

BACKSTORY

The **Bai Bei Shi Bank** is a new, ridiculously successful commercial and individual lender. Its investments prosper. Its rates of return are high. Its customer service is excellent.

The reason for the bank's success is simple. The building is perched on an emerging feng shui site, and the bank owes its prosperity to the dense flow of uncorrupted power. Several factions of the secret war therefore want to turn it to their own ends. The Architects of the Flesh, working through Triad agents, aim to ruin the bank's trustworthiness, then take it over.

The Man: The head of this Triad operation is named **Kim Sai Tu**. He's temporarily set up shop at a house in ritzy Victoria Peak, and called together a bunch of little brothers to do the dirty work. His Triad masters are calling the shots in principle, but in practice Tu has been working for **Denis Clech**, the Buro's head of security for contemporary Hong Kong. The two meet once a week at the **Chen Chien Building**, the Buro's HK headquarters, to discuss their plans. Tu and his Triad masters know nothing of the secret war, or who Clech is working for; as far as they're concerned, Clech is the head of a military technology firm named **High Start Industries** (with bogus offices in the Chen Chien Building) who is looking to get in good with the Triads. Clech says he wants the Triads' help in getting his company's products into new markets—namely, the criminal underground of Asia and the Middle East. That's a lie, of course; all Clech wants is a bunch of expendable mooks who will help the Buro gain power in Hong Kong while covering their tracks. Of course, he also recognizes the important role the Triad plays in HK and wants to benefit from their favors. (Clech and the Chen Chien Building are described in the Hong Kong chapter of the *Feng Shui* rulebook.)

The Plan: The Buro wants to take control of powerful HK feng shui sites, to aid in their expansion into this juncture. But they can't just send Buro tanks rolling into modern-day Hong Kong. So Clech hit on the idea of recruiting the Triads; they'd do the jobs and take the heat, and would have a vested interest in keeping things quiet. He's also counting on the Triads' paranoia and security to keep other factions from realizing just what the Buro is up to. Clech knows this won't last forever, but the quicker the Buro can gain ground in HK, the better off they'll be.

The current focus of Clech's plans is the Bai Bei Shi Bank. He's convinced the Triads he deals with that helping him take over a bank would be very useful to High Start's plans, and is sweetening the deal with a few arcanowave goodies for Tu and some others. The Triad members who are receiving AI/O port implants are excited at the novelty of these items; Clech, however, is tweaking each item he gives them to ensure that he can destroy them remotely if they fall into the wrong hands. He's also altered the arcanowave signature of each item so that it can be tracked; this makes the goodies unstable, but he plans on replacing them periodically for safety. Still, he's not taking many chances.

Initially, Clech is having the Triads harass the bank to diminish the bank's reputation and customer loyalty; later, they'll start leaning on the bank's owners and pressuring them to sell. He's also hoping to find ways to diminish the building's chi flow to further impair the bank's stability. Once it's wavering, he'll make the owners an offer they can't refuse, restore the chi flow, and the Buro will open for business as a financial mover and shaker in Hong Kong.

ABOUT THIS ADVENTURE

Brinks! is a short scenario, intended to kick off a new plotline in your campaign. It's extremely unlikely that the PCs will learn anything at all about the Buro's plan or about Denis Clech; at best, they'll snuff out a bunch of Triad thugs and maybe get Kim Sai Tu while they're at it. No clues lead to Clech or the Buro except for the two pieces of arcanowave technology that Tu and his men have, and those won't survive the adventure (though the PCs will get to see them in action). To the PCs, it'll be little more than a slam-bang bank robbery and some mook-wasting with a hint of something more; but in the process, they'll draw Clech's attention, and may quite possibly end up on very good terms with the managers of the Bai Bei She Bank. As your campaign continues, you can have Clech and the Triads continue to menace the bank—which will almost certainly draw the PCs back into the fray. Without realizing it, the PCs will have stuck their foot into an important Buro operation and made a powerful enemy. That's life in the secret war!

New PCs are suitable for this adventure, but may have some small problems of cohesion, particularly in that they're expected to track down the Triads and deal some justice once the immediate drama of the bank robbery is over. This is, perhaps, an ideal second scenario for a group of newly-minted PCs. More-experienced groups will mop up the situation easily and may know enough about the Buro's operations in contemporary Hong Kong that they can nail Clech on their own initiative.

GMC NOTES

Here are descriptions of the main GM characters in the story. There are more named Triad GMCs than are at all likely to come into play. Some can be used for the second scene. Only the leader carries extra ammo, so where a weapon can carry an extra round chambered, I've just added that in to its ammo total.

Den So Suk, attack leader

This Triad brother in his late thirties isn't too happy that he's still running street ops like this at his age, but he's never been respectful enough to rise far in the ranks. He gets on well with the little brothers who give *him* lots of respect, and so his superiors are happy to keep him down in the ranks, managing these sorts of operations to teach the little brothers the ropes. Of course, Suk isn't happy when he sees the same little brothers he taught rise up past him through the ranks.

Recently his life has become more interesting, thanks to his immediate superior and former protegé , Kim Sai Tu. Both Tu and Suk have had AI/O ports implanted in their bodies so they can use arcanowave gear, at the urging of Denis Clech. Neither know the first thing about arcanowave principles; they just know how to plug things in and use them. The surgery was done at the Chen Chien Building, though neither know that—they were brought there in secret. Suk's little brothers have taken to calling him Sukky Mnemonic behind his back, after the cyberpunk character in a recent movie, but they are impressed with the novelty of the implant and anxious to see what more it can do.

Den So Suk
Sample Dialogue: "Now you will all lie down on the floor and make no noise. If you think a bullet in the head will help you do this, we will be glad to oblige."
Attributes: Bod 6, Chi 0 (For 2), Mind 5, Ref 6
Skills: Arcanowave Device 6, Guns 13, Martial Arts 9, Intimidation 10
Arcanowave Schticks: Agony Grenade
Weapons: H&K MP5 K (10/3/30), one extra clip; Beretta 1201 riot shotgun (13/5/6)

The Ho Brothers (Lee Ha, Alan Tai, Kevin Do)

These three brothers are all the strong, silent type. Loyal to the death to their Triad masters, they would kill each other in a heartbeat if they had to. At present, their loyalty is particularly to Den So Suk. They know that Suk's little brothers often make it to the big time, and their only aim is to please him. The Ho brothers are callous in the extreme, and will not hesitate to hurt or kill anyone who even thinks about getting in their way.

The Ho brothers
Sample Dialogue: menacing glare
Attributes: Bod 5, Chi 0, Mnd 5, Ref 7
Skills: Guns 12, Martial Arts 9, Intimidation 9
Weapons (for each): Browning Hi-Power (10/2/14), Glock 17 (10/1/18)

The Kei Lee Brothers (Mao, Kai, and Kun)

Mao, Kai, and Kun are triplets; even Den So Suk cannot tell them apart. They have taken to wearing different colors of suits, but each triplet always wears the same color. They've taken on the *nom de plumes* of Mr. Brown, Mr. Blue, and Mr. Black (same color as their suits), inspired by the gangster flick *Reservoir Dogs.* The Kei Lees have an uncanny instinct for sticking together and knowing when the other triplets are in danger; this is reflected in their Chi score. At your discretion, the brothers can even see through each others' eyes in moments of crisis, though they are not aware of this even happening—they just know where to aim and shoot to save one another without even thinking about it. The trio are loyal to each other first and foremost, and they're inseparable. They have a habit of finishing each other's sentences, or saying the same thing at the same time.

The Leman Brothers (Stephen, Carlton, Robert)

These expatriate mafia hoods are on loan from the Kansas City mob in America. They're cooling their heels in HK for a month or so while their bosses are having some big meeting. Since the Triads have insisted on providing security for the meet (it's their turf), the Lemans have been cut loose to hang out with the little brothers. They liked the idea of a bank robbery (the mafia never does cool stuff like that anymore, it seems) and got in well enough with Den So Suk to do the job. The Leman boys' bosses will blow a gasket when they find out their "kids" were out robbing a bank, but the Lemans are irrepressible—they just want to shoot guns and have fun. They're all slightly-naïve Missouri hicks, much more cowboy than gangster. Still, it's hard not to like them. Suk has been careful not to let them in on anything to do with Clech or the arcanowave goodies. As far as they know, this is just a heist.

Unnamed Triad Goons

Some of these guys are the next generation of Hos and Kei Lees. For now, though, they're just dime-a-dozen mooks.

GETTING STARTED

It's up to the players to decide why the PCs are at the Bai Bei Shi Bank. They may be inside or outside the bank—but it's preferable for at least some of the PCs to be inside. They may do their banking here, or may be meeting a contact. Perhaps there's something in a safety deposit box they need to retrieve, or they need to put something in one for safe keeping. Law-and-order PCs with Triad contacts may have been tipped off to expect "trouble" at the bank today; they might even be tailing the Leman brothers in the hopes of finding out where the Mafia-Triad meet is going down.

SCENE 1: THE BANK

The bank building fills a block in the heart of the Wanchai district. It rises squarely for ten stories, then splits into four towers aligned with the points of the compass. The square floors are partitioned internally as shown on the map on the next page.

The bank occupies all ten stories (and the towers) of one quadrant, with the main entrance at street level. The other three quadrants are occupied by offices.

The bank's streetfront is entirely glass, supported by decorative copper pillars. The other two walls alternate expensive wood paneling and mirrors.

In the center of the bank's space is a triangular atrium rising ten stories to a translucent skylight. A red-carpeted staircase follows the atrium's border, opening onto balconies and the bank's administrative and managerial offices.

Resting on the ground floor, directly beneath the atrium, are two two-story pieces of machinery. A coin-dispensing teller machine has an elaborate network of ramps, wheels, chutes, and the like through which change can be sent rattling in an entertaining fashion. A bill-dispensing teller machine has robotic arms which can fold bills into origami designs.

Teller windows and a vault fill up one wall, customer service cubicles the other. A bank of elevators occupies the center of the building, where the interior walls converge.

The Kei Lee brothers
Sample Dialogue: "What he said!"
Attributes: Bod 6, Chi 1, Mind 5, Ref 5
Skills: Guns 11, Martial Arts 8
Weapons (for each): Remington 870 Police (13/5/7), Desert Eagle .357 Magnum (11/3/11)

The Leman brothers
Sample Dialogue: "Watch it, gook! Uh, no offense, Suk."
Attributes: Bod 6, Chi 0 (For 1), Mnd 4, Ref 5
Skills: Guns 10, Martial Arts 7
Weapons (for each): Two Colt 1911As (10/2/8)

Unnamed Triad Goon
Sample Dialogue: "When do we eat?"
Attributes: Bod 5, Chi 0, Mnd 4, Ref 5
Skills: Guns 8, Martial Arts 6, Intimidation 8
Weapons (for each): Uzi (10/4/40), Colt Detective Special (9/1/6)

Bai Bei Shi Bank Security Guards
Sample Dialogue: "Drop your—" *BLAM* "—agh! I'm hit!"
Attributes: Bod 5, Chi 0, Mnd 5, Ref 5
Skills: Guns 7
Weapons (for each): Colt Detective Special (9/1/6)

Bai Bei Shi Bank Armed Customers
Sample Dialogue: "I'm no hero—just an average joe with a gun."
Attributes: Bod 4, Chi 0, Mind 5, Ref 4
Skills: Guns 6
Weapons (for each): one of American Derringer Mini Cop (11/1/4), Auto-Ordnance Pit Bull (10/1/8), or Grendel P-12 (9/1/13)

Unarmed bystanders have the same stats, apart from the weapons.

Other details are left to player and GM improvisation: planters, counters for filling out paperwork, spinner racks of advertising material, etc.

AN ARCHITECTURAL NOTE

The Bai Bei Shi Bank owes a great deal to the real-world Bank of China Tower, as described in *Hong Kong Architecture: Aesthetics of Destiny*, edited by Vittorio Magnago Lampugnani, Prestel-Verlag, 1993, ISBN 3-7913-1324-X.

Getting Things Started: The adventure begins in the midst of business. Lines queue up for each teller window. A crowd surrounds the atrium teller machines. The PCs can plausibly be anywhere on the ground floor, or passing by outside.

The bank security staff consists of four guards on the ground floor (two at the entrances, one at the elevator, one circulating through the crowd), and two more patrolling the upper levels. They strongly discourage open displays of weaponry, and warily watch anyone who seems to be packing concealed heat.

A delivery of funds is going on. There is an armored car parked outside, with an armed driver and escort. Two men carry bags of money, escorted by two more armed men.

How Many Triads: There should be a named Triad character and two to three unnamed Triad goons for each PC. Pick them from the GMCs provided earlier before the combat starts.

ACTION!

Suddenly, a bunch of massive black sedans pull up outside. One zooms in front of the armored car, disgorging armed mooks who gun down the armored car driver and escort. The others pull in behind it, and more mooks pour out. These charge through the front doors (apart from a dramatically-minded few who pause to shoot out windows and leap through the voids).

In their first few shots, the attackers aim to take down the security guards. Next they plan to intimidate the crowd into lying on the floor while the goons sweep up all readily accessible loot, inflict random property damage, and leave. Killing anyone not actively resisting isn't part of their plan; general harassment is. They do not reckon on any serious opposition.

Faces in the Crowd: In addition to the player-characters, there should be about a half-dozen unnamed defenders among the bank crowd (about one per player-character). If any of the player-characters are unarmed, put defenders nearby and have them killed early on, conveniently dropping their weapons.

Significant opposition throws the attackers into confusion. They cluster together. Some try to grab the high ground of the atrium staircase. Others shelter in cubicles. Others grab any convenient cover, which in one or more cases should include human shields.

THE BAI BEI SHI BANK

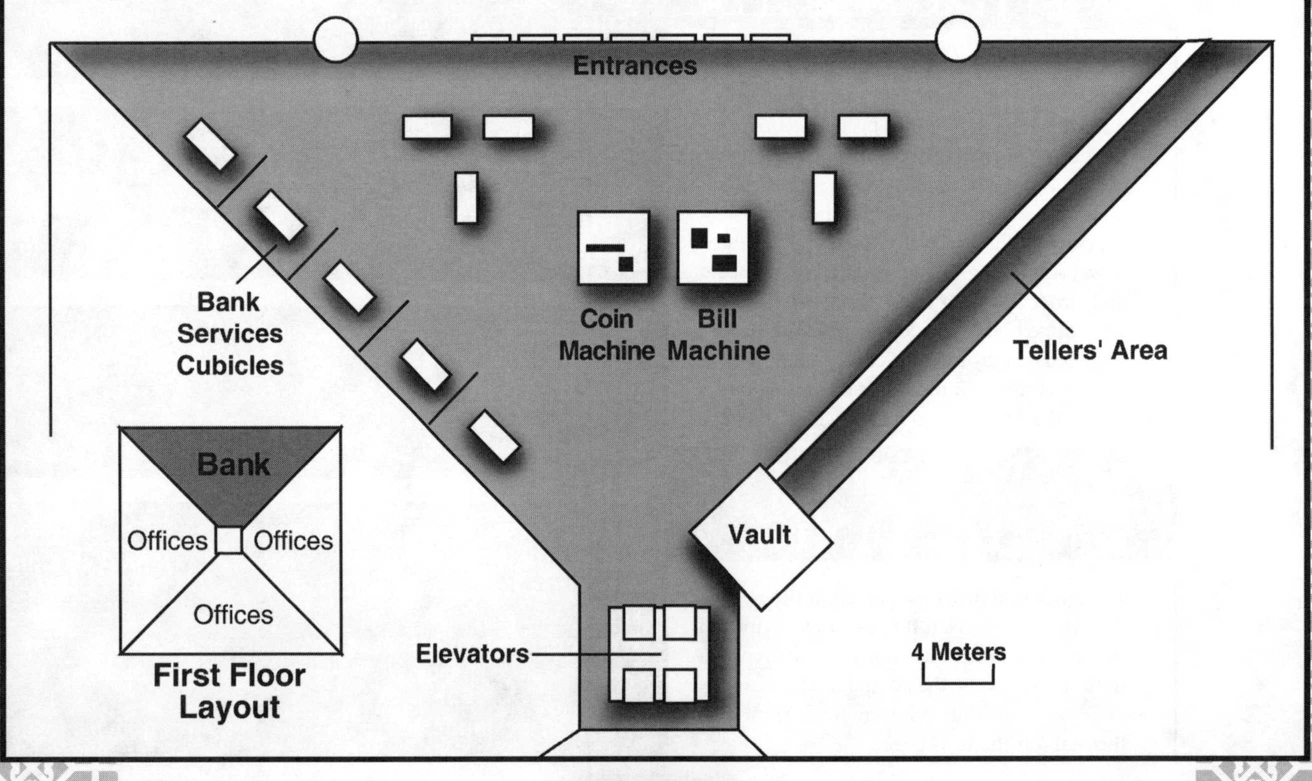

Sukky Mnemonic: Den So Suk is itching to try out his agony grenade. He knows enough to use it like a regular grenade—in other words, don't be near it when it goes off. Chances are good that he'll throw it behind him when he and his little brothers make their exit, so that the PCs and any other pursuers get the hurt put on them. You can find rules for the agony grenade on **p. 144** of the rulebook. Suk's only got one, but it's already charged up and ready to go so he doesn't need to muck around with his AI/O port during the robbery. When the grenade goes off, it disintegrates—but any PC with Arcanowave Device skill knows that some sort of Buro weapon was used, and may even specifically recognize it as an agony grenade if it seems appropriate.

NEAT THINGS THAT COULD HAPPEN

- The fancy teller machines will inevitably take damage. When either takes four points of cumulative damage, it begins to malfunction. The coin dispenser spews a fountain of change all around. Trying to move faster than a slow walk within two meters of it becomes increasingly difficult: a Difficulty of 3 the first sequence this happens, rising by 2 every sequence thereafter. The bill folder's arms begin swinging wildly, attacking one randomly-selected target within three meters each attack. They have Brawling 4, Spd 3, and a damage value of 5.
- The lobby has the usual velvet ropes supported by heavy, free-standing metal posts. The posts make good clubs; with the ropes still attached, they can even trip someone up if thrown properly.
- A handful of deposit slips from one of the counters can be thrown at someone's face, blinding them momentarily and fouling their aim; this could be considered a defensive action.
- If a hand-to-hand fight breaks out around one of the paperwork counters, one of the high-quality fountain pens chained to the counter can be driven through someone's hand, 'penning' them to the counter.
- The red carpets that lead to the offices and other bank areas can be yanked, sending assailants tumbling.
- The numerous bystanders will be a problem. They get underfoot, or panic and get shot in front of an anguished PCs' eyes. For extra pathos, have a blind old woman stumbling around in frightened confusion, constantly wandering into the line of fire but never quite getting shot.

WHACKING ON THE TRIADS

When half the attackers are down, the others suffer a -1 AV morale penalty. When only four are left, the survivors flee, aiming for the nearest of their cars and zooming off.

FOLLOWING IMMEDIATELY

By far the most efficient course of action is for the PCs to rush out after the fleeing goons. Chances are that not all the cars that arrived will be leaving, since a bunch of mooks are probably gushing blood all over the carpeted lobby. The cars were left running, so it would be a simple matter for the PCs to pile into as many sedans as it takes and set off in hot pursuit.

This course is strongly to be encouraged. If the GM wants to add some playing time and complications, the chase can be played out, with competition for lanes, high-speed cornering on narrow mountain roads, and the like. Or the GM can simply cut to arrival at the Shaw home and begin the next scene.

FOLLOWING LATER

One way or another, at least one PC should find out where the surviving goons are going. This could be done by interrogating dying mooks (a gun in the mouth is a powerful incentive) or using magic to get the info.

Any dying mooks with info on the tips of their tongues croak before the police arrive. The complications of dealing with the law could conceivably get intricate: the GM should feel free to shortcut these proceedings if PCs aren't up to (or interested in) them. If the PCs did in fact manage to save the day somehow, the bank officials are deeply appreciative, and intercede with the police.

Sooner or later (preferably about the time of a dramatic sunset), the PCs are again at liberty. If they haven't yet decided to go after the other goons, they should be encouraged, prodded, or otherwise motivated to do so. If nothing else, if any named GMCs died, the rest will come back, hungry for revenge. Their attack is up to the GM, but should again provide an opportunity for the PCs to question the wounded or follow the fleeing. One way or another, they should get to the next scene.

SCENE 2: THE HOME

Chek Shaw was a rising star in the Ministry of Finance, successful enough to build a home in the style of Southern California architecture he'd admired as a student at UCLA. Unfortunately, he was better at running corrupt side dealings than concealing them. When scandal broke, he committed suicide, a few weeks before play begins. The Triads moved in and took care of the paperwork necessary to use his home as a temporary base of operations. Kim Sai Tu—Den So Suk's boss—is the guy in charge here.

It's a two-story building perched on a steep north-facing slope. The only ready access is along a curved quarter-mile driveway, leading to an entrance in the upper story. The carved iron gates that used to close the driveway have been sold off, leaving the way open (apart from the goons who keep surveillance). Those willing to do some scrambling, however, can climb up the side of Victoria Peak, reaching an open concrete utility bay directly beneath the lower floor. From there a support pillar leads up to the living room balcony. There's a risk of detection, though: a Difficulty of 5, and it takes three sequences to make the climb from a convenient turn-out along a road lower on the hillside.

The ceilings are low throughout the home except in the vaulted living room. Walls are dark wood paneling hung with classical Chinese art; floors are hardwood with expensive Persian rugs draped around. The furniture is plush. Electronic gadgetry proliferates.

The upper-story entrance leads to a hallway running the length of the floor, with the floor given over to bedrooms and a storage room full of Shaw's boxed worldly goods awaiting disposal. A broad staircase leads downstairs.

The bulk of the lower story is an enormous living room and dining area. To one side is the kitchen and pantry. To the other is Shaw's office, now used by Kim Sai Tu, and a sauna. Tu is in the office when the PCs show up, brooding over the robbery and his next moves.

Two guards keep a constant eye on the driveway, and are in radio contact with the de-facto command post set up in the living room. Two more circulate through the grounds. Eight more guards are taking it easy in the living room or sauna, three shots' worth of action away from their weapons. All of these are unnamed goons as described in the statistics for the first scene. There are also four named henchmen, to be taken from the first scene statistics as well. Two of these are working on plans with Tu, two are part of the relaxing crowd.

Any survivors of the bank attack are recuperating in the kitchen, snarfing down munchies.

Enough sedans to carry the goons, four to a car, are parked outside.

Kim Sai Tu, Triad Brother

This ambitious Triad brother is in his early thirties, a few years younger than Den So Suk but farther up the career ladder. He's smart, but easily riled when his little brothers screw things up. Should the PCs encounter him in a non-violent situation, he's constantly rubbing his neck—that's where his AI/O port is, and it itches constantly.

As noted in the description of Den So Suk, Denis Clech had Suk and Kim Sai Tu get AI/O ports so he could encourage their loyalty with some minor arcanowave toys. Tu is more than a little leery of the port and the gear, unlike Suk who sees opportunity in everything. Still, Tu has

HOUSE

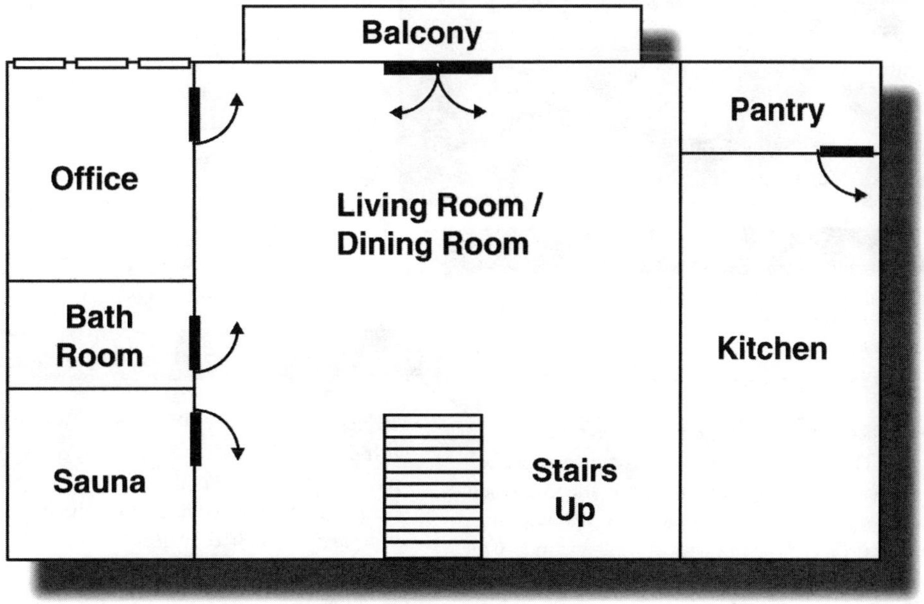

LOWER FLOOR

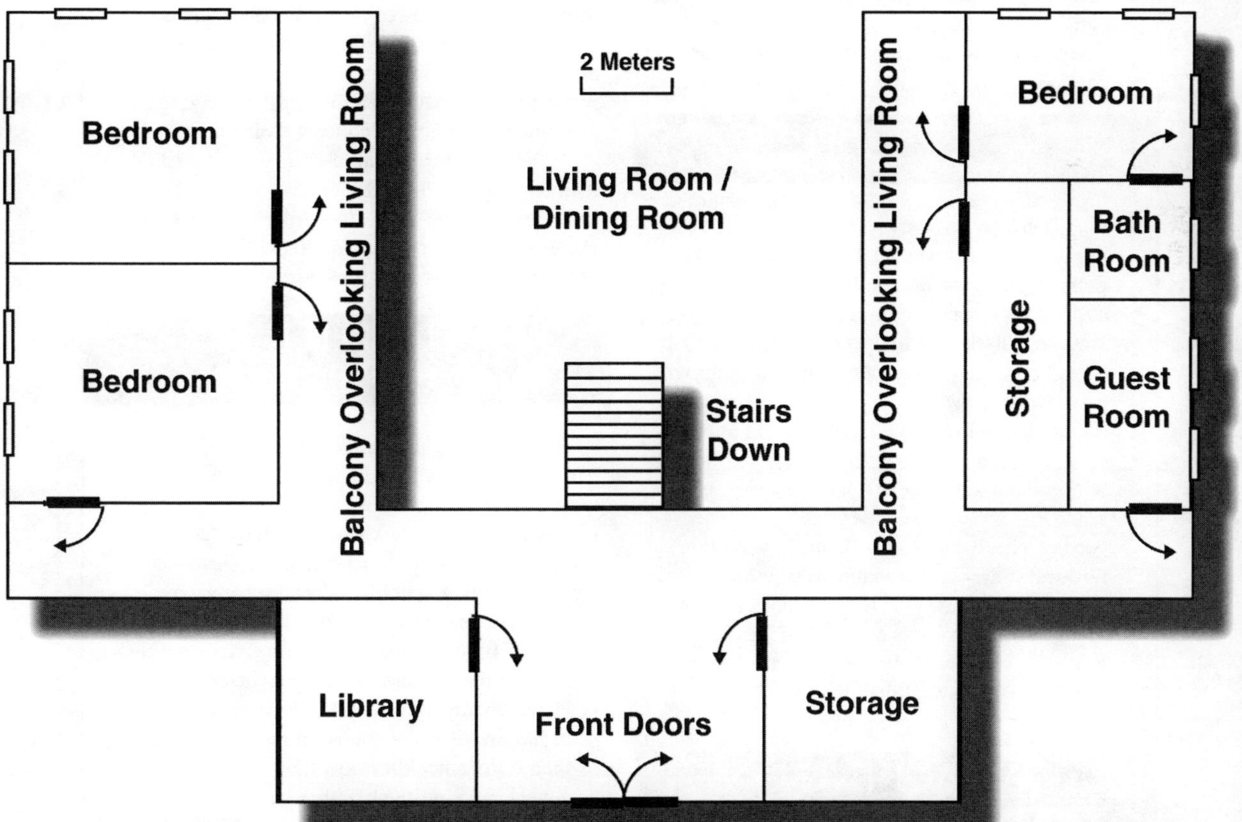

UPPER FLOOR

tried out his Aerial Mobility Unit a few times and thinks it's the cat's pajamas. He won't hesitate to strap it on and go zooming off a balcony if the battle is going poorly.

Kim Sai Tu
Sample Dialogue: "I am surrounded by incompetents! I lose face when these lumps bungle my plans!"
Attributes: Bod 5, Chi 0, Mnd 7, Ref 7
Skills: Arcanowave Device 6, Guns 14, Martial Arts 11, Intimidation 12
Arcanowave Schticks: Aerial Mobility Unit
Weapons: Colt 1911A (10/2/8), one extra clip

ACTION!

When the alarm is given, all but the two henchmen and Tu converge on the reported location of trouble. If a second alarm is given, the guards split up, and Tu and his henchmen join the force moving on the second interruption.

The rest of the scene is a room-to-room battle. Feel free to add more mooks to the mix whenever you like, and work in some drama with the named GMC brothers who are still around; if the PCs waxed any of the Kei Lees or the Lemans, the survivors will be out for blood. The house is big, with lots of rooms, doors, and windows, so the PCs never know where the next mook is going to come from. If you've seen *The Killer,* think of the battle at the safehouse after the assassination, where all the white-jumpsuit mooks show up and come crashing through every entrance in sight.

NEAT THINGS THAT COULD HAPPEN

- There are so many possibilities here that it's impossible to list them all. Just look at which room in the house the combat is occurring in, and see what comes natural. The kitchen will have big pots, knives, and canisters of flour that can all be used against opponents. Bedrooms will have dresser drawers to hurl at people, closets full of clothes to hide in, and pillows to muffle shots during a stealthy intrusion. And so on. Keep in mind that the house is full of heavy, expensive knick-knacks such as statues, vases, and other goodies. Nearly anything a PC might want to throw at someone is probably close at hand.
- With so many gun-happy mooks running around, friendly fire is a real possibility. Once a mook blows away a fellow little brother by accident, the PCs may get the idea and try to encourage more crossfires like that.

WHACKING ON THE TRIADS, AGAIN

As at the bank, the goons suffer a a -1 AV penalty when half their number are down and they try to flee when just four are left. They try to set the home on fire as they leave, if this is at all convenient.

If Tu is one of the final four, he grabs his Aerial Mobility Unit from a convenient hiding hole and zooms off. The flight should be emphasized: the strangeness of the device is intended as a tip-off to the PCs that more is going on than they had previously realized. If Tu is down, one of the goons still standing tries to use it but, lacking an AI/O port, can't make it do a thing; as soon as the PCs see him with it, the device explodes, killing the goon and doing grenade damage (see p. xx of the rulebook). Clech realized that Tu was dead and that the plan was in trouble, so he activated this AMU's custom self-destruct option.

WRAPPING UP

The gentry of Victoria Peak don't care to put up with this much random violence (except, of course, when it's dramatically interesting). The police arrive a few minutes after the last of the goons are dispatched or flee.

Whatever loot the attackers made off from the bank with is at the Shaw home. This makes the bank officials very, very happy, and earns the PCs a significant debt of gratitude. The police are naturally curious about the whole thing but can be cowed by Bai Bei Shi Bank contacts among their superiors. Ascended agents among the cops are particularly interested in reports of the AMU, though they'll make at least a rudimentary effort to conceal their interest.

The adventure, or at least the action part of it, ends with the characters released to go about their own affairs again. The bank promises each character a reward equal to a month's income of whichever character is richest.

FURTHER ADVENTURES

- As noted earlier, the PCs have earned the bank's favor. They now have trustworthy contacts there.
- The Triad are displeased. The characters come under occasional surveillance. If they interfere with another operation, they'll become prominent targets. Pay special attention to their interactions with Triad members in other scenarios in this book, since those situations may be worsened if the PCs have already hacked off the Triad.
- The Architects of the Flesh have an interest of their own, since they now have to come up with new lines of attack on the bank. (In turn, these generate requests for help from the bank.)
- The Ascended are also interested, especially once they've clued in to the bank's good feng shui. The Pledged cops will suspect the PCs of knowing more than they're telling.

A television bolted to a dresser is the initial focus of our attention. Looking at the rest of the room, we see the walls are dirty, the beds are rumpled, and the table is littered with boxes of take-out food. Drawing the eye, however, is a startling assortment of munitions: pistols, shotguns, sub-machine guns, magazines, boxes of bullets, packs of explosives, timers, and other goodies. Three people sit on the beds, fussing with the weapons and half-watching the television. They are: MING JIAN, a friendly-looking Chinese-American woman in her early thirties; BIG JIM SLADE, a big, buff, intense martial artist who's also good with guns; and DEREK "SHAKY" WILLITS, an aging and crazed Vietnam vet and demolitions expert.

TELEVSION NEWS ANCHOR

—no leads as yet, though police confirm they have received numerous letters and threats from the so-called "Temple Fist" terrorists. The group's bombing campaign is only two weeks old, but with three major explosions and more threatened, Hong Kong is on edge. To date, no demands or motives have been offered—nor has any suggestion of when the terrorists will strike next.

DEREK "SHAKY" WILLITS

(fingering a block of C-4 explosive)

About three hours from now, Miss TV Lady. Boom!

BIG JIM SLADE

(turning off the set with the remote control)

Cut that talk, Shaky. You never know who's listening.

SHAKY

(mocking)

But we're staying in the Big Comfort House! Big Comfort they promise, Big Comfort we get!

MING JIAN

That's enough. This terrorist ruse is working so far, but it could also get us into Big Trouble if a maid hears us talking like this. Jim, I want you to head outside and make the block. See if anybody's watching the motel. Be careful.

BIG JIM

Yes, ma'am.

BIG JIM picks up two .50 Desert Eagle Magnum pistols, checks them, and shoves them into twin holsters under his heavy jacket; then he leaves.

SHAKY

You sure about this demon stuff, Miss Jian? Rikki Ko's Ultra Fine Pizza don't look like no evil temple.

MING

I'm sure, Shaky. Come dusk, they'll be spinning pizza for the demon lord Eng Fan Mei.

SHAKY

(attaching fuses)

Okay by me. Long as I get to blow some demons up.

MING JIAN picks a shotgun off the bed and walks over to the window. She sees BIG JIM outside, making the rounds.

MING

You will, Shaky, you will.

(picks up shotgun and jacks a shell in)

When the sun goes down, Eng Fan Mei goes down too…

GREG STOLZE

BLOOD FOR THE MASTER

ILLUSTRATED BY DAVID FOODEN

Premise: The PCs hear of terror tactics being used to scare people out of a neighborhood.
Twist: The "terrorists" are trying to scare people away and attract police attention because a temple of demons is going to materialize—the more human combatants and the fewer non-combatants, the better.
Climax: The PCs chase a demon and hostage into the temple, kick butt, and possibly end up sent to the future.

BACKSTORY

Many years ago in China a foul temple was cursed for its evil and depravity. Though its crime is long forgotten, **the Temple of Eng Fan Mei** is still remembered, its name synonymous with demons and horror.

Of course, part of this infamy may be due to the nature of the curse. The entire Temple was torn out of the countryside and set adrift in the Netherworld. Now, whenever the energies of a location line up just wrong, Eng Fan Mei can appear in our world for a single night. Desperate to escape their prison, its repulsive denizens boil forth—unless they are stopped.

(Cue up the theme music, 'cause here's where your PCs come in.)

An American geomancer and demon fighter named **Ming Jian** is the only outsider who is aware of the Temple of Eng Fan Mei. For the last couple of weeks she has arranged three bombings in Hong Kong: one in a closed bakery, one at a construction site, and one on a boat (which she had purchased on the black market). The first two were attempts to realign the area's chi flow in order to prevent the Temple's appearance. When that didn't work, she blew up the boat for effect, and claimed responsibility in the name of a terrorist organization called "The Temple Fist" (which she made up completely). She has sent a series of rambling and cryptic letters to police and media. She also videotaped the boat bomb from a safe distance and sent these tapes to local TV stations. Predictably, it's gotten a *lot* of air time. She plans to blow up the place where the temple is going to appear, so as to disperse civilians and draw the authorities' attention just before the temple arrives. That way, she hopes, Eng Fan Mei will meet some stiff opposition when he comes cruising in.

Exposition: To set this up, your PCs should all be aware of the "Temple Fist Bombings." Violence is the coin of the realm in *Feng Shui* Hong Kong, but no one seems to know who the Temple Fist are or what they actually want. The police are always "pursuing leads," but nothing seems to come of it. What do a boat and a bakery have in common? No one seems to know, just like no one knows when Temple Fist will lash out next.

GETTING STARTED

"Blood for the Master" was designed as a beginning scenario—there's nothing like a crisis to rope together disparate plot elements! It can also be used to introduce slightly more-experienced characters to time travel and the Netherworld.

The neighborhood of Yaumatei in Hong Kong is aligning (or maligning) chi forces powerful enough to turn **Rikki Ko's Ultra Fine Pizza** (carry out only) into the Temple of Eng Fan Mei—for one night. The PCs can have any number of reasons for being near Ultra Fine Pizza on that fateful night:

- Picking up a favorite garment next door at Rikki Ko's Right Sharp Cleaners. (Rikki has an ancient Chinese secret for getting out tough stains like blood.)
- Cops of any stripe will have heard rumors about Temple Fist terrorists stirring up trouble.

Ditto Masked Avengers, ditto anyone who associates with Triads.

- The neighborhood has any number of gambling dens, hole-in-the-wall herbal pharmacies, massage parlors, bars, cut rate women's shoe stores—all sorts of enticements for anyone who isn't too stuck up about the presence of thugs, prostitutes and homeless madmen.
- Rents in this area are comparatively reasonable; it's not a swell place to live, but it beats having your face chewed by rats under a bridge.
- It's also a great neighborhood for vigilante crime fighters to go spill some bodily fluids.

And the number one reason...

- Ultra Fine Pizza!

GMC NOTES

Here are descriptions of the main GM characters in the story:

Ming Jian, Geomancer and Demon-Hunter

At 5'5", Ming Jian doesn't look like a terrorist (which she really isn't) or a kung fu expert (which she really is). She is also a geomancer, sufficiently attuned to the flow of chi to recognize the poisonous growth that's about to erupt like a pimple from hell in the middle of Hong Kong.

Saving the world from demons is pretty time consuming, but in her off hours she teaches Asian History at Syracuse University. Raised in America by Chinese parents, Ming had some cultural troubles in the past, but since she dedicated herself to justice, they have bothered her much less. After all, there's nothing like deadly combat with otherworldly evil to put things like "Mom and Dad just don't understand MTV" into perspective.

Although she knows the traditional behaviors her native culture demands, and can play the role it would demand of her, she is more comfortable "acting American." Left to her own devices, Ming is cheerful, extroverted and sometimes a bit of a clown.

Big Jim Slade, Ming's Right-Hand Man

"Big Jim" was a nickname given to James Slade by cruel classmates. Overweight and asthmatic, Jim took up yoga seeking relief from his breathing problems. It provided him much more; his yoga instructor sensed that Jim's chi was a powerful resource, waiting to be tapped. Once in touch with his inner energy, Jim's physical problems evaporated. He began studying the martial arts with Ming primarily for their focus on internal energy—the fighting aspect was secondary to him. He's become Ming's right-hand man in her war on demons. Jim has a degree in computer science, but he works as a temp in order to leave time free for helping Ming.

Calm and methodical, Jim's tranquility strikes many as icy; but though he controls his emotions strictly, they are still there. Foremost among them is his loyalty to Ming. For all his composure, Big Jim is practically a fanatic.

Derek "Shaky" Willits, One Severe Whacknut

Shaky didn't do too well in Vietnam—'nuff said? Though a classically-trained demolitions expert, Shaky's tendencies to twitch, tic, mumble and stammer out long and pointless sentences about nothing in particular have prevented him from reaping the peace dividend of his skills. He was the best that Ming could get a hold of on short notice (what do you expect? She's a college professor, not a Mafia assassin), and both she and Big Jim watch him closely.

Not closely enough, however; Shaky habitually carries enough C4 on his person to level a large building, along with a dozen or so dynamite sticks to impress those who aren't sophisticated about explosives. It's *all* wired to go; if threatened, Shaky will laugh in an unnerving manner, throw open his coat, and stutter his way through an appeal to his opponent's self-preservation instincts. Ming and Big Jim will be just as surprised by this as anyone else.

Ming Jian
Sample Quote: "I don't suppose you've seen any hellspawn around here, have you?"
Attributes: Bod 6, Chi 1, Kung Fu 8, Mnd 5, Ref 10
Skills: Martial Arts 15, Guns 13, Info/Geomancy 7
Schticks: Hands Without Shadow, Dim Mak, Lightning Fist, Natural Order
Weapons: Punch (7), Kick (8), Bernadelli Shotgun (13/5/10), Ruger K89 (10/2/15 + 1), Sig-Sauer P-220 (10/2/9 + 1)

Big Jim Slade
Sample Quote: "Make a better choice."
Attributes: Bod 9, Chi 0, Kung Fu 8, Mind 5, Ref 6
Skills: Guns 9, Info/Computers 9, Martial Arts 12
Schticks: Natural Order, Willow Step, Hands Without Shadow, Both Guns Blazing
Weapons: Punch (10), Kick (11), Uzi (10/4/40), Two Desert Eagle .50 Magnums (remember, he's hunting demons) (12/3/9 +1)

Derek "Shaky" Willits
Sample Quote: "Whoa, I'm sweatin' like dynamite in a hot mine shaft here..."
Attributes: Bod 5, Chi 0, Fu 4, Mind 5, Ref 5
Skills: Driving 12, Guns 14, Martial Arts 10, Sabotage 12
Gun Schticks: Eagle Eye, 2 Hair Trigger Neck Hairs, Signature Weapon
Weapons: Punch (6), Kick (7), 5 bombs (a nice c-4/dynamite cocktail with a white phosphorous chaser—damage 12-27 depending on proximity, conceal 2), Grendel P-30 (signature weapon, 8+3/1/30 + 1)

Lt. Liu Gow, SWAT Team Commander

His troops are drilled harder, yelled at more and disciplined with greater relish than any other unit in Hong Kong. Most of them love Commander Gow for it.

Liu is about as implacable and fearless as a human being can be. His emotions work for him, not the other way around; he's hard to fool, hard to distract, and impossible to bluff. All in all, a formidable opponent. The Ascended have an eye on him, but have not yet attempted to rope him in.

Unfortunately, when things get tight, Liu will probably wade in and assume that anyone who looks like trouble is a terrorist.

Rikki Ko, Impulsive Entrepreneur

Rikki is something of a staple in Yaumatei: his pizza-stained brown suits, cheap cigars and pervasive aroma of cheap cologne are familiar almost everywhere.

In addition to the pizza place and the dry cleaners, he also runs Rikki Ko's Video Paradise, Rikki Ko's Authentic British Suits For Men and Rikki Ko's World of Wigs. In addition, he has a significant interest in the popular No More Troubles Liquor Store.

In fact, Rikki pulls down about a cool million every year, after taxes and protection money. You'd never know it to look at him; he's a very hands-on manager and routinely puts in 14 hour days hopping from business to business in a 1988 Oldsmobile Cutlass. At ten he may be helping to inventory new movies at Video Paradise, only to dash off to ease the lunch time rush at the pizza place or oversee the assembly of some "authentic British suits." It's remarkable that he's had the time to father six children.

Rikki has the business instincts of a shark and more energy than a 14 year old boy on a hot date. Sadly, he has absolutely no impulse control at all. His ability to think on his feet has served him well as a businessman, but may do less well in a firefight; he's equally likely to charge in, guns (ineptly) blazing, or to give any enemy a great view of his worn down Hush Puppy heels.

Surprisingly, Rikki is liked and trusted in the business world—possibly because he is absolutely incapable of deceit. Even his rivals respect the fact that he'll tell them right to their faces "You know, if you were drowning, I'd throw you the anchor. Seeing your face makes me want to spit up. I'm going away, my heart can't stand looking at you."

He carries an enormous gun in a shoulder holster, just in case one of his businesses gets robbed while he's there. He's never drawn it in anger; not because of any moral compunctions, but because it just never occurs to him. His first reaction to anything unpleasant is to yell at it and keep yelling. His family lives in a rather tasteful home in the Southside, selected and decorated by his wife Yu-Li. His children are almost utterly unlike their father (who, after all, was absent for most of their upbringing), taking instead after their mother who is beautiful, understated and classy—everything Rikki isn't. This applies doubly to his eldest daughter, Linda.

Characters who save Rikki's life, or who at least tried to save the pizza place, may earn his gratitude. This is a double-edged sword; Rikki has money, and thinks of himself as generous to friends, but it's a stingy man's generosity. He's more likely to send presents of liquor, suits and pizza than actual cash. In return, he'll make a big, embarrassing deal of the characters, who will soon be widely known by everyone in Yaumatei. If Rikki knows where they are, it won't be a secret—and anyone who wants to get at them might realize they could kidnap Rikki.

8 Nameless Cultists, Death in a Hairnet

Unknown to Ming (or anyone else) the cult of Eng Fan Mei is alive and well. Eight of its members (and that's most of them) have taken jobs at Ultra Fine Pizza. When the Temple appears, they intend to sacrifice someone to Eng Fan Mei as soon as possible and then glory in the rewards they've been promised for years.

Lt. Liu Gow
Sample Quote: "Over the top, boys—move move *move!*"
Attributes: Bod 6, Chi 0, Mnd 5, Ref 7
Skills: Guns 14, Martial Arts 10, Police 9, Leadership 10
Schticks: Both Guns Blazing, Lightning Reload x3
Weapons: Mossberg Special Purpose Shotgun (13/5/9), Auto-Ordnance Pit Bull (10/1/7 + 1), AMT Automag V (12/3/5 + 1), punch (7), kick (8)

20 Nameless SWAT Team Members
Sample Quote: "Yes *sir!*"
Attributes: Bod 7, Chi 0, Mind 4, Ref 6
Skills: Guns 8, Martial Arts 7
Weapons: Sig-Sauer P-220 (10/2/9 + 1), Colt M6351 SMG (10/5/32) or Mossberg Special Purpose Shotgun (13/5/9), punch (8), kick (9)

Rikki Ko
Sample Quote: "First my tax bracket goes up, now this! I might as well just shoot myself and spare destiny the effort!"
Attributes: Bod 4, Toughness 8, Chi 1, Mind 4, Ref 5
Skills: Guns 4, Martial Arts 3, Info/Hong Kong Entrepreneurs 16
Weapons: Colt Anaconda (11/3/6), Pizza Knife (7), punch (5), kick (6)

Eight Nameless Cultists
Sample Quote: "Blood! Blood for the Master!"
Attributes: Bod 6, Chi 1, Mind 4, Ref 6
Skills: Guns 7, Martial Arts 7
Weapons: Glock 17 (10/1/17 + 1), Pizza Knife (9), punch (7), kick (8)

ON LOCATION

Rikki Ko's Ultra Fine Pizza is in a large building, sharing a wall with **Rikki Ko's Right Sharp Cleaners** on the right and a strip bar called **Bootytown** on the left. (Rikki owns the building, but isn't a partner in Bootytown; he doesn't hold with strippers. In fact, he frequently justifies his rent increases by admitting that he's trying to drive them out of business; however, business stays resolutely good—possibly due to the talents of Trisha the Tigress of Trenton, New Jersey, their Saturday night main attraction.) Ultra Fine Pizza is a bustling business (take out only) known for fast, if surly, service. Rikki is a loud, overweight man who chews unlit cigars. He is completely unable to prevent himself from yelling out whatever happens to be on his mind at the time. For some strange reason, Fast Eddie's men don't blow him away for saying things like "Oh, more gangsters again? Coming in like bloodsucking ticks for your protection money? Well, I suppose I better pay up before you shoot me point blank in the crotch!" If asked about this, Fast Eddie's little brothers attribute it to the entertainment value.

The neighborhood around Rikki Ko's Ultra Fine Pizza is a rich and varied one. Well, it's varied, anyhow—the only "rich" thing about it is possibly the smell.

Rikki Ko's Right Sharp Cleaners has strong competition from **Jane Wong's First Rate Cleaners** up the street. (Just look for the sign that says "Ladies! Leave your pants here and enjoy the afternoon!") There's a rumor that Jane had a curse put on Rikki Ko. After the Temple appears, Fast Eddie and his pals will quietly stop asking Jane for protection money, figuring that he can damn well protect himself.

The notion that Jane Wong has truck with the supernatural may have something to do with his upstairs neighbor, **Roy Marker**. Roy is a round-eyes private detective—owner in full of the **Citizen Arcane Detective Agency.** Rumors abound about Roy, claiming that he's everything from a disgraced FBI agent, to a defrocked priest, to the living incarnation of Satan. For sure, he's a spooky-looking guy with tattoos on his wrists. From the amount of ordnance he's flashed at various times, it looks like he's a lifetime NRA member as well.

For those who don't like gwailo food, there's a sushi bar around the corner. The name spelled out above the door indicates something like **Food That Has Mercifully Avoided The Damaging Flame Awaits Your Mouth.** Someone with a sense of humor translated this to **Eat Me Raw** in English.

In the basement of the Damaging Flame (as its more tasteful patrons call it) there is a high-stakes illegal casino. Fast Eddie has protection

© 1996 David Fooden

up the wazoo around this place. It's simply called **Risk** and is notorious in Hong Kong; for every person who's actually been there, there are hundreds who've heard of it. In Risk, you can not only gamble your money, but your life as well; **Chef Motosune's** specialty is fugu ovary soup. Fugu fish are deadly poisonous, but if the poison can be diluted enough, it provides an ecstatic buzz. However, there's a fine line between "too little" and "enough to kill you." Most fugu dishes straddle that line, but cooking the ovaries is so dangerous that it's illegal in Japan. Chef Motosune does far better than most; only 20% of those who eat the soup are instantly killed. (It's rumored that the sign translator was fed raw fugu 'till he croaked before Fast Eddie decided he liked the joke.)

Fugu can also be used to produce a "death-trance" so complete that coroners can be fooled. This may be part of the explanation for the sudden (and highly convenient) "death" of Fast Eddie's "identical twin" (Fast Donald) in 1987, followed by Fast Eddie's equally sudden appearance.

High rollers have been known to offer to forgive stunning debts if the loser agrees to order the soup. Some of these losers then become psychologically addicted to the fugu thrill.

Other losers, however, simply pawn their prized possessions at **Queen's Knight Pawn**, open 24 hours for your convenience, one short block away from Risk. (Just look for the eerily sexy portrait of a young Queen Elizabeth in the window.) Queen's Knight Pawn is a long, narrow, dusty store full of the weirdest bric-a-brac imaginable. They've got more than repossessed VCRs and the guitars of disillusioned teenage rockers; Roy Marker claims they once had a *possessed* VCR. There are jars in the back containing things that look like they were once alive, but couldn't possibly be... right? The proprietress, **Gong Yip Chu**, claims to have sold everything from a rare root that actually screamed in daylight, to one of the legendary Seven Dragon Balls. (She says that it was number 3 and that she got took by a fast talking Brazilian named Braulio because she didn't realize what she had.) Even if you don't believe her, it's worthwhile to listen to her stories.

SCENE 1: RUMBLE IN THE ULTRA FINE

The PCs are hanging around Yaumatei when all hell breaks loose (figuratively—literally comes later). This takes place about an hour before sunset. Ming, Jim and Shaky have been casing the pizza place for quite a while—Ming and Jim for traffic patterns, Shaky for structural weaknesses.

Ming knows the transformation will occur at sunset, and she wants as few innocents around as possible. Therefore, she and Jim plan to storm Rikki Ko's half an hour beforehand. This will have several effects: it will give Shaky

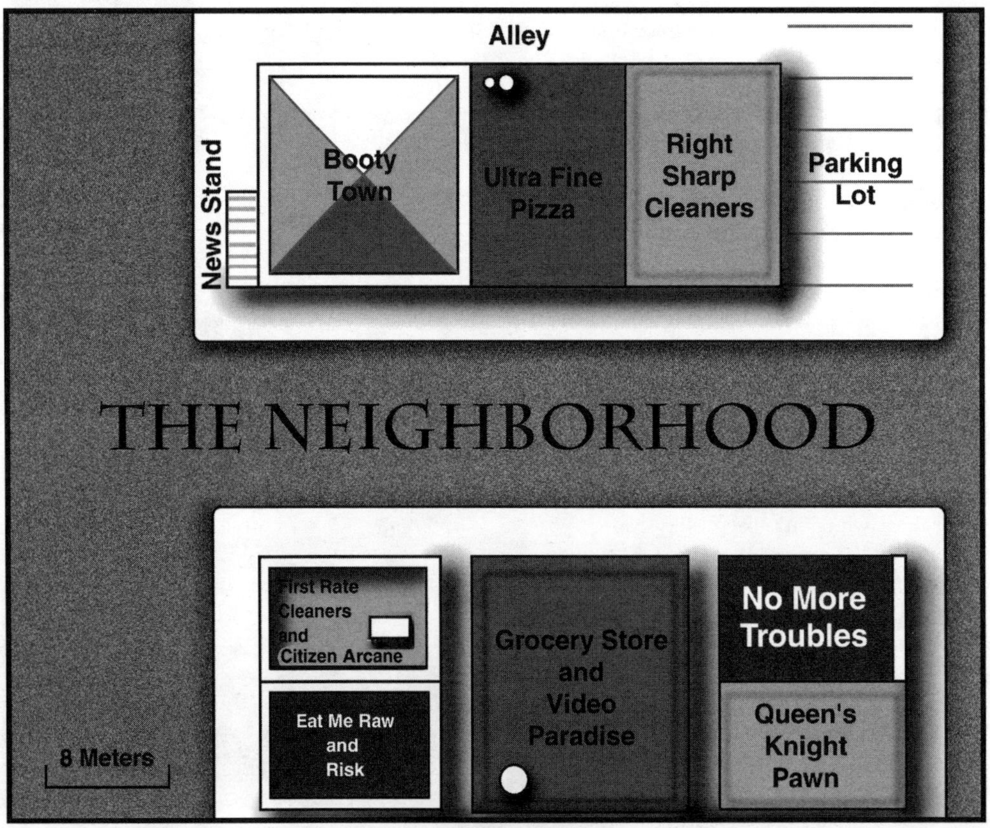

time to mine the building, it will bring in a whole lot of firepower, and it will hopefully rid the area of bystanders.

What Ming and Jim don't know is that the **Nameless Cultists** are planning to take over fifteen minutes later.

ARRIVAL OF THE "TERRORISTS"

At least one PC should be in or in front of Rikki Ko's when Ming and Jim walk in from the cleaners next door, both carrying large garment bags. Once inside, they unzip them to reveal not a besmirched Armani or wine-stained ballgown, but an UZI (for him) and a Bernadelli (for her). They'll drop the garment bags and stand over them (there are magazines, shells and their other guns inside).

The plan is for panic to ensue as people try to escape. They have no problem with this; they *want* the cops to show up. Shaky is in the building when they enter, and he will behave as if he doesn't know them; that is, scream, cower and hide behind the counter.

What they aren't expecting is Nameless Cultists and PC-sized trouble. When Ming and Jim whip out the guns, there's the 30 or so seconds of screaming and yelling that they expect. Then, however, all the Nameless Cultists pull out their guns and start trying to jump-start the apocalypse.

To PCs, this is going to be a tad confusing; one minute, they're picking up a pizza, the next they're dodging bullets. Have fun with it. Ming and Jim will (initially) attempt to use non-lethal Fu power attacks on the pizza goons; they'll figure they're just normal (if rather well-armed) folks trying to defend their livelihood. They'll start to get lethal when they realize these pizza assemblers are yelling things like "Eng Fan Mei will suck your boiled eyeballs!"

The cultists are plain blood-bonkers loons. They'll try to kill whoever they can, as quickly as possible. Both factions are likely to think that intervening PCs are enemies, though the cultists are more likely to attack them unprovoked.

NEAT THINGS THAT COULD HAPPEN

- Pizza cutting knives are large and sharp, but that's too obvious.
- Fresh, hot pizzas can be thrown, frisbee fashion, to engulf the heads of unfortunate cultists. Ouch! Burning hot sauce!
- There's a soft drink case out front that can readily be pulled over, shot or smashed. It's the old-fashioned kind with a glass door and metal racks full of soda bottles.
- In back, there are two large, high temperature pizza ovens with conveyor belts. Pizzas go in one end raw and come out the other end cooked. A person might just fit on that belt... the belt is something like a metal mesh, so watches, handcuffs, necklaces and rifle straps can easily be wedged in to pull in unfortunate cultists/cops/characters.
- Blood-red chunky sauce is kept in huge plastic garbage cans in back. It's slippery and ready to spill. The garbage cans are on wheels to move them around more easily.
- The beater for the pizza dough is not sharp, but the twin, interlocking blades move fast and

ULTRA FINE PIZZA

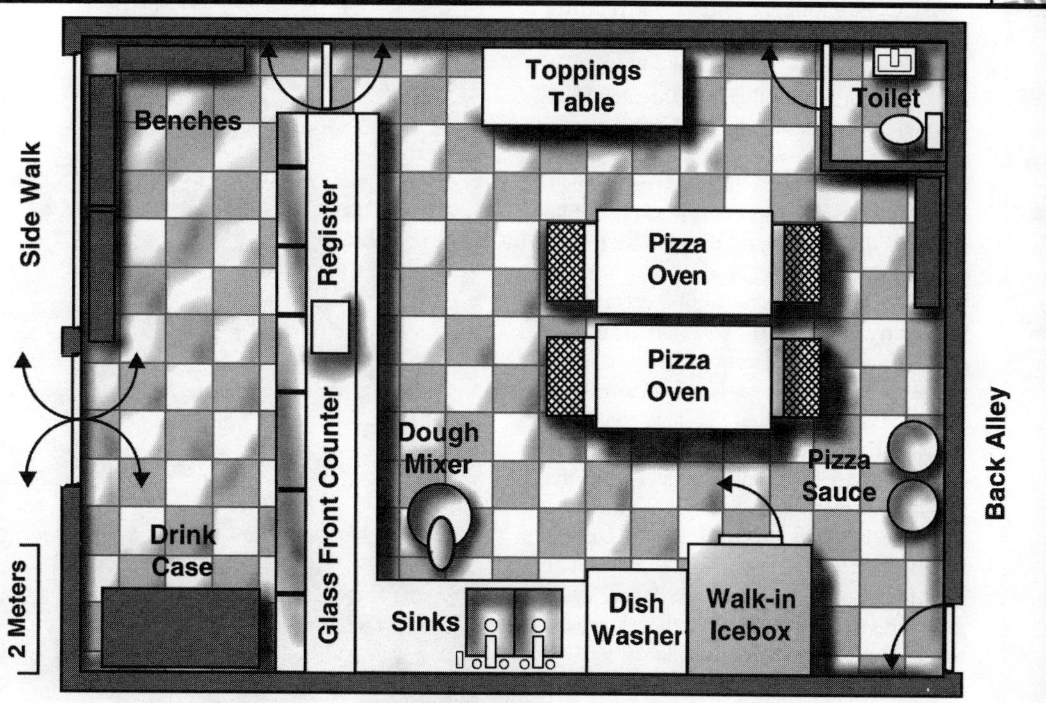

are about two feet long, six inches wide—ready to become a whirling deathtrap.

- The dishwasher sterilizes with live steam, plus chemicals strong enough to burn your eyes out.
- The sink has a hose attachment, which could work some mischief when combined with the fact that the lights are all bare bulbs hanging on cords—just begging to be broken.
- There's a walk-in freezer in one corner. Inside are stick salamis about three feet long and an inch thick—frozen solid, they make swell cudgels.
- The mixer bowl for the dough is stainless steel, on wheels, and is large enough for a person to kneel in. Kneeling, it provides about 50% cover. Standing, maybe 25%.
- The cash register is large, heavy, and will come up "no sale" if someone is whacked with it.

WHACKING ON THE WEIRDOS

There are a number of possible results for this kitchen combat.

The PCs and Ming's company kill the cultists: This is probably the best outcome. If this is how things are shaping up, have one of the Cultists get a "lucky" shot on Ming and leave her bleeding and gasping. As she dies (probably in Big Jim's arms) she'll gasp out a dramatic description of what's going to happen to the PCs.

Then **Liu Gow's** men show up—just in time to keep Shaky from mining the front wall of the store. If the PCs are relatively unharmed, you may allow the SWAT team to just start filling the shop with supersonic lead for a while, then have it turn into the Temple.

The PCs and the cultists kill Ming's company: This might as well read "The PCs Kill Everybody," because that's what will happen; at some point, a PC or cultist will threaten Shaky, who will do his flasher move. The PCs can try to juggle this one any way they want, but it's going to take some very fast action and/or talking to keep Shaky stable—especially if Ming and Jim are dead. Shaky will want to demolish the building, and the Cultists will *not* allow it. You can play through the standoff until it gets boring, or the PCs try to change the equation. If they attack the cultists, the SWAT team arrives just as Shaky is placing his last charge. They will attempt to trap the PCs like rats and negotiate Shaky into defusing the bomb. (Good luck, lieutenant.) This can lead to a second standoff—and when that gets boring, the Temple appears.

The PCs get the hell out of Dodge: If your PCs are weasels who want to stay out of a good fight just because they aren't sure who the good guys are and it's none of their business, they'll probably enter the Temple without any bruises, contusions, splinters, etc.; good for them.

© 1996 David Fooden

However, if they bug out then they'll get caught in a huge mob of Yaumatei natives with the same idea. They could make a get-away if they're willing to break the skulls of innocent civilians or pull some wonky Fu trick like Prodigiously Leaping up onto a nearby building—but they still will be around for the arrival of the SWAT team and the destruction of Ultra Fine Pizza.

HERE COMES TROUBLE

Without PC intervention, the Cultists over-power Ming and Jim, and Shaky goes ballistic. The resulting explosion will kill off the rest of the Cultists and blow the pizza place to the mainland—or it *should.*

Instead, before the amazed eyes of the PCs and the SWAT team, the bricks will fly up, only to get sucked back down into a new configuration, a huge and malign structure of pillars, gables, and wonkin' big doors.

Before they see the temple, however, they'll just see a bunch of smoke and a few maimed Cultists or bystanders crawling dazedly away. Then they'll see a scaly and non-human hand reach out of the smoke and grab an aforementioned dazed crawler. The smoke will clear, revealing the temple. The PCs should see the Cultist or bystander being dragged in for maybe two seconds before the door slams shut.

If Shaky's bomb doesn't go off, the pizza parlor just morphs into the temple as described above, only without the explosion. Make this happen whenever you feel like it. If the PCs are inside the pizza parlor when the temple arrives, adjust the description of "In The Temple" (p. 22) accordingly. They'll see the walls shift around them, etc., but will not be harmed by the process. It's just more up close and personal than if they're out in the street with the crowd.

SCENE 2: THE ULTRA FINE TEMPLE OF ENG FAN MEI

Now that the temple is here, it's time for some demon-whacking. Here are our ready-made targets:

Ten Bloodhunter Demons, Servants of Eng Fan Mei

Bloodhunters are unnamed demons who serve Eng Fan Mei. This primarily means finding victims to stuff in his mouth. They're not too bright, but they're quick and nasty. Before Eng Fan Mei is awakened, they'll attack anyone weak and defenseless-looking, trying to grab him or her for delivery into the belly of the beast. After that, they'll launch suicide attacks on anyone who looks dangerous to their Master.

Bloodhunter Demon
Sample Quote: "Me gnaw skull!"
Attributes: Bod 8, Chi 0, Mnd 3, Ref 8
Skills: Creature Powers 10, Martial Arts 8
Schticks: Abysmal Spines x3, Flight, Regeneration x3
Weapons: Claws, fangs and pointy things on the tips of their wings & tails **(15)**

Eng Fan Mei

Eng Fan Mei looks like a big, particularly ugly statue. This is what he is—until a living victim gets put in his mouth. Then he's a big, particularly ugly, moving, firebreathing, kill-crazed statue.

Before being "awakened," Eng Fan Mei will be squatting in the middle of the temple. Picture an iron statue of a 20 foot tall, naked sumo wrestler. Add a few pounds. Contort the face into a hungry grimace of rage full of sharp iron teeth. Add four curved, flamelike horns sticking up from the top of his head, and a series of about six eyes down the line of his spine—and there you have Eng Fan Mei.

The mouth and eyes (both the ones on the face and the ones on the spine) are open hollows. Looking into one on the back (if a character is lucky or dumb enough to try this when Eng Fan Mei is dormant) will reveal that the statue is hollow, and has a pretty thick layer of charred, crunched up bones in the bottom. Once someone is stuffed into Eng Fan Mei's mouth, however, the entire statue will become filled with fire, casting an eerie glow from the eyes and mouth. Plus, he starts rampaging around killing people.

Eng Fan Mei
Sample Quote: "Gwaaaaaaah!" (Insert sound of background screams.)
Attributes: Bod 15, Strength 20, Chi 2, Mnd 5, Ref 8
Skills: Creature Powers 15, Martial Arts 15
Schticks: Regeneration x3, Blast (Fire). In addition to his "normal" regeneration, Eng Fan Mei can decrease his wound points by 5 simply by eating a person or a blood hunter.
Weapons: Four pointy horns, about ninety pointy teeth, huge trampling feet and big honkin' fists (21), Fire (17—shoots from mouth or eyes, including the eyes on his back, depending on Eng Fan Mei's mood; all his moods are "bad," but there are subtle variations.)

ON LOCATION

There are basically two ways the PCs can play this: smart 'n' wimpy, or dumb and gutsy. If they're dumb and gutsy they'll charge into the temple, draw the attention of the blood hunters and maybe prevent Eng Fan Mei from being awakened. If this is the course they pick, check out "In the Temple," below.

If they opt for the wimpy selection, then the blood hunters boil out of the temple, followed by Eng Fan Mei, doing a rather credible Godzilla impersonation. If they allowed this to happen, go to "Fightin' in the Streets," p. 24.

CAREFUL WHO YOU EAT!

If Eng Fan Mei eats someone who is carrying a loaded gun or a full clip, all the bullets will go off in his stomach. Each bullet or shell will do full damage—soaked by his toughness of 10, of course, but this does mean that dropping or throwing a fully-loaded Mossberg shotgun down his throat will do 27 points of damage to him after toughness. (For the mathematically-minded, here's how that's figured: each shot does 13. Subtract 10 'cause he's made of iron, you get three. Multiply that by the nine shells in the rifle, you get 27). This does mean, oddly enough, that feeding him a cop's handgun (Sig-Sauer P-220 with 10 bullets doing 11 damage), is more damaging than when he eats a cop's submachine gun (a Colt M6351 with 32 bullets doing 10 damage—all of which is soaked by his toughness.)

Do not tip your characters off about this! If Eng Fan Mei eats a cop or an armed character, you can describe the ringing "boom" and the dimples that appear in Eng Fan Mei's belly. That's clue enough.

Remember that no matter how brutish he acts, Eng Fan Mei is not dumb. Once he recognizes that guns and clips are painful to eat, he will take care to not eat them.

IN THE TEMPLE

The temple of Eng Fan Mei is a long, dark chamber with a 30' ceiling and balconies on either side. At the far end of the chamber, the balconies turn into sweeping staircases that cross in the middle, forming a landing ten feet up before coming all the way down to the floor.

Framed by the stairways squats Eng Fan Mei. Two columns of pillars begin with the ends of the stairways and go to the doorway at the front of the temple, forming a sort of open corridor. The columns alternate between being wide at the bottom and tapering upwards, or wide at the top tapering down. They are an ivory white and are nastily reminiscent of fangs. There are four columns in each row.

Between the columns and slightly inward are large bowls full of flaming oil. These bowls are about two and a half feet wide and shallow—much like giant woks. Their red flames cast a bloody, flickering light upon the temple.

At the end of the temple, squatting between the first two columns, is Eng Fan Mei.

If the characters have charged in right away, they might be able to intercept the one blood hunter who is dragging a victim towards the statue; but if they try this, the other nine will swoop down from the balconies and begin a lovely donnybrook.

NEAT THINGS THAT COULD HAPPEN

- Half of the pillars are wide enough to use as cover, but that's too simple by far.
- A character who gets up on the balcony can leap off, grab a narrow column and slide down, slowing as it widens.
- The stairs have banisters, wide enough to slide down head first (as if sledding) standing up (as if skateboarding) or straddled (as if… well… sliding down a bannister!).
- The banisters are supported by thin stone columns about a foot and a half apart. If someone

ULTRA FINE TEMPLE

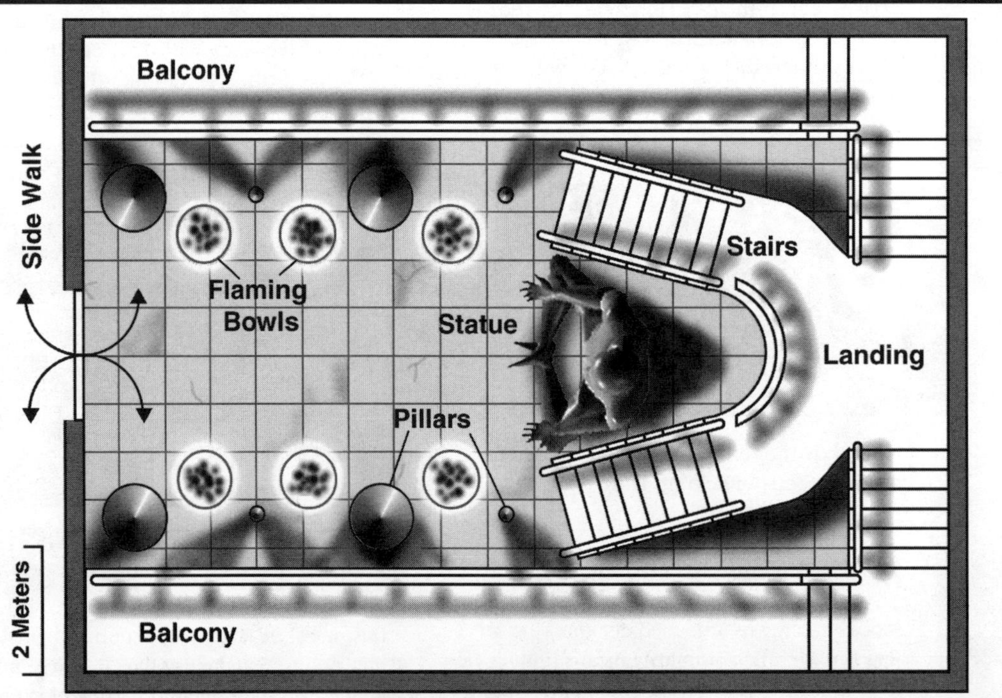

on the banister or the stairs is being dived at by a blood hunter, he or she may be able to drop down suddenly and trick the demon into smashing head-first into the bannister. If this happens, the demon's head will get stuck between columns.

- The shallow bowls of burning oil are easily tipped over, spreading slippery fire across the floor. With a running start, this can be skated across like ice, or even slid into to send up a splattering sheet of burning liquid.
- If someone shoots the far edge of an oil bowl just right then it will flip, sending a flaming curtain into the air. This is real effective against flying blood hunters.
- The bowls can also be picked up and used for a "pie in the face" attack as the Marquis de Sade might have directed it. It's a tricky (difficulty 4) stunt to pick one up and fling it like a discus, spewing flaming oil in all directions as it flies, hitting a blood hunter at the end, and not setting oneself on fire. Striking with the edge of an oil bowl does strength +4 damage, or +6 if it's thrown. The oil does 15 points of damage per turn if someone is doused with it, or 5 per turn if they're only spattered or have only an extremity on fire. When in doubt, characters are spattered, bad guys are doused.
- Pillars can be destroyed if they take 20 damage to their narrow end or 40 damage to their wide end. This damage cannot be from burning, but it can be from fu strikes or explosives. All damage done to pillars by firearms is halved (though something like a rocket launcher would do full damage). The easiest way to knock out a pillar is, of course, to trick Eng Fan Mei into punching or kicking it, or to put one of Shaky's bombs at the narrow end. If two pillars that are next to each other in a row or across from each other are destroyed, the roof between them caves in, doing 30 points of damage to any and all beneath. You have a choice to make if your characters destroy more than two adjacent pillars; if you feel like it, this lack of structural integrity may sufficiently change the chi flow that the temple is once more set adrift in time—with the characters inside. Or not, depending on how you feel like playing it.

WHACKING ON THE BLOODHUNTERS

Once the characters and the demons have exchanged a few blows, evaluate the combat and, if necessary, adjust events a little bit. There are several ways the combat can go:

The PCs kick mucho boo-tay: If your characters are treating blood hunters the way airline employees treat luggage and have kept Eng Fan Mei dormant, you may opt to have Lt. Gow and his snarling commandoes come charging through the door, guns blazing indiscriminately. If

this happens, it is quite possible for a blood hunter to grab one and wake up the big guy. Alternately, if your characters are already pretty beaten up and it seems like a good time to end things, you can let them finish off the blood hunters unopposed and take a brief respite before the Temple gets shelled. (See "An Ultra Fine Adventure" on p. 25.)

Toe-to-toe slugfest: If the characters and the blood hunters seem equally matched (with or without Eng Fan Mei), you can choose to let things continue until it becomes clear that the situation has shifted to one of the other two possibilities.

The PCs fold faster than Superman on laundry day: If they've been getting bad rolls or making less-than-completely-adequate decisions, they may well be getting folded, spindled and mutilated by Eng Fan Mei and his minions. In this case, Lt. Gow and company can burst through the front door and show a bit more discretion with their firepower, saving the collective butt of your party. In this case, everyone will probably get clear of the Temple before it departs. (See "Wrapping Up" on p. 25.)

FIGHTIN' IN THE STREETS

If the PCs don't charge into the temple as soon as it appears, the blood hunters will awaken Eng Fan Mei, and they'll attack as a group. This is not a good thing. The blood hunters will swoop out of the door first, followed by Eng Fan Mei.

On the plus side, Lt. Gow and his bully boys will be present to fill the sky with flying lead. Their presence will essentially give Eng Fan Mei an automatic 7 wound points per sequence. In addition, at the beginning of every sequence, roll one die and consult the handy chart below.

HANDY COPS-KILLING-DEMONS CHART

Roll	Bloodhunters Slaughtered
1	2
2-3	1
4-6	0

On the down side, there is a straight 50% chance every turn that any character approaching Eng Fan Mei or his minions will be mistakenly shot at by a hot-headed cop. Check this on each character's first action.

NEAT THINGS THAT COULD HAPPEN FOR ENG FAN MEI

- Eng Fan Mei may choose to pull up a street light and use it like a golf club on the cops or the characters. His swing does 25 damage, so look out.
- A dozen or so scantily-clad male and female strippers have fled Bootytown and are at the back of the screaming, fleeing crowd. Naturally, the blood hunters will pick these attractive individuals as sacrifices to their master.
- The first time Eng Fan Mei flame-blasts a car and it blows up, he'll be surprised (and possibly hurt, if he blasts one close by). After that he'll use this to his advantage.
- Eng Fan Mei could trample a fire hydrant, gushing water all over the street and creating a powerful spray.
- There is a large crowd of fleeing bystanders. If they get gridlocked (and if Eng Fan Mei isn't defeated pretty quickly, they will be) the big iron demon will wade into the middle of the crowd (killing many), sit down (crushing more) and start stuffing people into his mouth.

NEAT THINGS THAT COULD HAPPEN FOR THE PLAYERS

- If a PC can shoot through a power line and drop it onto Eng Fan Mei, the electricity will do 10 points of damage that cannot be stopped with his toughness. If a fire hydrant has been opened to provide really good conduction, this damage will be doubled.
- Severed power lines are only dangerous if you're going to conduct the energy, either to the other severed line or to anything touching the ground. Characters who leap up, snap a power line and swing on it Tarzan-style may be able to shock Eng Fan Mei a good one—assuming that they bail out before the line strikes, of course. This does mean that one end of a line will not harm a flying blood hunter. (GMs who want to use cinematic physics in this scene can assume that the power lines will work in whatever crazy ways the PCs expect them to.)
- A refrigerated delivery truck has been abandoned with the keys in the ignition. It's got a full tank of gas and is loaded with various foodstuffs for the pizza place. If it is rammed into Eng Fan Mei it will do 20 damage (actually 10 with his toughness) and will (of course) explode, spilling freon, food and tomato sauce all over the place. The resultant surface might cause Eng Fan Mei to slip and fall (5 damage after his toughness—the bigger they are, the harder they fall).
- He's even more likely to fall over if the food/freon sludge is wetted down with water from the fire hydrant.
- If the PCs can somehow trick Eng Fan Mei into biting into the refrigerated back of the truck, the cold freon pouring into his superhot interior will kill him outright. However, Eng Fan Mei isn't dumb; it'd better be a superlative trick.
- The blood hunters have never seen clear glass. Like birds, they will think it's empty space

and may fly straight into it if characters are behind it (for example, inside cars.)

- Across from the former-pizzeria-now-infernal-temple is an alley which is too narrow for Eng Fan Mei to fit down. The buildings on both sides are lined with fire escapes, and strung between them are countless laundry lines, so it's hard for blood hunters to swoop down in the alley. This makes a great sniper post—at least until Eng Fan Mei decides to clean it out with fire.
- There are quite a few cars parked on the street. If a character can get Eng Fan Mei to trample one or fire-blast it, it will go up—possibly damaging the demon or a blood hunter flying above it.

WHACKING ON ENG FAN MEI

If the characters hesitated, and the street was their battlefield, a lot of bystanders die. It's unavoidable, and it's up to the GM to decide how detailed to be in describing the shot and trampled victims.

If Eng Fan Mei is killed before all the blood hunters die, the blood hunters will fly off. If Eng Fan Mei and all the blood hunters are kacked, a great ragged cheer will rise up from the crowd, the temple will vanish, and the characters will be feted as heroes—for a while.

On the other hand, if the characters are defeated (or even worse, run away) large, heavily-armed choppers will sweep into the area. Civilian casualties will be heavy as Eng Fan Mei is bombed into oblivion at the command of the Ascended's Pledged police choppers. (If my characters wimped out and ran, I'd sic 'em with nightmares forever, but maybe I'm just vicious.)

WRAPPING UP

If Eng Fan Mei escaped the temple, the Ascended will quickly put "Operation Acid Rock" into effect. Regardless of whether the demon was defeated by the characters (Yaaaay!) or by the merciless butchers of the Ascended (Boooo!), strangely silent choppers will fly overhead spraying everyone beneath with a highly psychoactive chemical. You may choose to play this out for your characters, or they might avoid it if they're lucky or skillful. Things will get very strange. (Play this up—visions of lost loves, strange hints about the future, nightmarish battles with old enemies—go ahead and freak your character's minds, but keep the tone weird and dreamy so that the fight with Eng Fan Mei remains the definite climax.) When everyone's head clears, Eng Fan Mei, the temple and the bodies of the blood hunters are gone; in their place are gruff people in unfamiliar blue-grey uniforms, and many paramedics.

The official explanation is that the Temple Fist bomber detonated an "LSD Bomb," and that any reports of silent black choppers, flying demons and big iron statues are all mass hysteria. If you play this right, you may have the characters doubting it all—until that one blood hunter that survived tracks them down, thirsty for revenge…

FURTHER ADVENTURES

- What about those guys in the blue-grey, and those silent black helicopters? This foray into *X-Files* territory will bring the characters into conflict with the Ascended.
- Investigation of Ming Jian may put the characters in touch with people who can lead them into the Secret War—especially if they hear about the Temple and what the characters can do.
- Those eight psychos in hairnets were 80% of the Eng Fan Mei cult. The remaining two were sorcerers who were well aware that their ass-kicking demon king was going to feel a bit snacky when he emerged. When they learn that their master was killed thanks to a bunch of meddling kung fu do-gooders or cops, they'll come looking for vengeance.
- If Ming, Jim or even Shaky survived, they may ask the PCs to help hunt down demons.

AN ULTRA FINE ADVENTURE

If the characters defeat Eng Fan Mei inside the temple, or kill the blood hunters before Eng Fan Mei can be awakened, they may get a unique opportunity: the chance to have a building get shelled around them! That's right; once the Ascended get hip to what's going on, they'll try to bomb the Temple back to the stone age (though in fact, they'll only bomb it forward to the Buro.) Once the structure of the Temple is changed enough, its unique feng shui patterns are disrupted and it's once again sent into the Netherworld.

This disruption may also occur if the characters and/or Eng Fan Mei do enough damage to the building. The temple will be "in between" in the Netherworld for a while; the specific while is up to the GM. It can be as long as several hours (allowing the characters to leave, return, possibly leave again—whatever) or as short as ten shots before it leaves the Netherworld and emerges in a grocery store in 2056.

The possibilities here are wide open for GM creativity, but here are a couple of ideas:

- If the characters are still fighting the demons and are doing poorly, they can get rescued by warriors in the Netherworld. You'll need to determine who these warriors are and what their interest in the temple is. Perhaps it's a batch of Lotus mooks trying to seize the temple and bind Eng Fan Mei to their will. Perhaps it's agents of the Buro who know the temple is en route to 2056 and want to settle Eng Fan Mei's hash before he arrives. The PCs shouldn't get off scot-free if you send in the cavalry.
- If the characters leave (or flee) the temple into the Netherworld, they could end up in the domains of any of the Four Monarchs. If you're a cruel GM, they might show up just as an attack is mounted by another faction, which the characters can either aid or thwart.

The eunuch sorcerer GAO ZHANG, leader of the Eaters of the Lotus and secret ruler of ancient China, has just summoned PAI LAI, Demon Lord of the Six Agonies, into his richly-adorned chambers. The demon appears in a flash of smoke and fire; he's ten feet tall, with a serpent's head and glowing eyes.

PAI LAI

You dare to summon me, human?

GAO ZHANG

I did summon you, Pai Lai. Of all the Demon Lords of the Underworld, you alone have not paid respect to my court.

PAI LAI

And why should I respect you or your court, you castrated oaf?

GAO ZHANG

Because I lead the Eaters of the Lotus! Because I rule all of China! Because demons dance at my command!

PAI LAI

Don't get too full of yourself. Your Eaters of the Lotus are nothing but a gaggle of pathetic eunuchs who play at sorcery. I would rather be the lowest of peasants than King of the Eunuchs!

GAO ZHANG
(enraged)

You do not give me face!

PAI LAI
(coolly)

It is *you* who do not give *me* face. You order me, a demon lord, to come to your chambers. You expect me to pay you respect. Where is your respect for me, Gao Zhang? No, you will get no face from me. And if you call me again, you will regret it!

PAI LAI disappears in another flash of smoke, leaving GAO ZHANG fuming.

GAO ZHANG

Impudence! Treachery! I will not stand for this treatment!

GAO ZHANG strides over to a great archway and bellows at several GUARDS standing in the hall.

GAO ZHANG

Summon the Inner Council! We have a matter of honor to discuss.

GUARD
(quivering)

Is—ah—is there anything we should tell them to better prepare for the meeting?

GAO ZHANG's eyes narrow. He reaches into a pouch at his belt and hurls a handful of powder at the GUARD, who bursts into flames and disintegrates in seconds. The remaining GUARDS cower and bow.

GAO ZHANG

You may tell them I am not in the mood for questions.

CHRIS PRAMAS

PAI LAI

ILLUSTRATED BY DAVID FOODEN

Premise: A disgruntled Buro scientist urgently needs the PCs' help in stealing a magical artifact from the Buro and freeing a feng shui site.
The Twist: He's actually a Jammer, and plans to destroy the site—and the PCs, if they don't get out of the way.
The Climax: The site serves as a prison for an ancient demon lord who isn't exactly in a good mood, and the PCs are the first thing he's had the chance to kill in centuries.

BACKSTORY

In 66 AD, **Gao Zhang**—leader of the Eaters of the Lotus—made a new enemy. **Pai Lai**, Demon Lord of the Six Agonies, had refused to give Gao face and had insulted both Gao and the Eaters of the Lotus. Gao Zhang, unused to being thwarted, had thought long and hard about his revenge. He didn't want to simply kill Pai Lai; death was too fast and easy. He wanted Pai Lai to really suffer, to suffer for so long that he forgot what it was like not to suffer. Most importantly, he wanted Pai Lai to know at whose hands he met his fate.

The following year Gao Zhang lured Pai Lai to a potent feng shui site. Pai Lai thought that Gao had learned his lesson and would now show him proper deference. He was wrong. Gao instead planned an ambush. He and his eunuch minions attacked and magically bound Pai Lai inside the feng shui site. Then Gao enacted a ritual to seal the feng shui site forever. The last thing that Pai Lai heard was the mocking laughter of Gao Zhang; then he was alone in the darkness.

The feng shui site was sealed and Gao Zhang made only one key. He kept this key on his person at all times, lest his enemies free the enraged demon lord. History does not record what became of the key after the eunuchs were swept from power.

THE HOOK

The key remained lost for almost 2,000 years. However, it has just been uncovered at an enormous strip mine run by the Architects of the Flesh in 2056. The engineers running the mine had no idea what they had found, so they called in a science team. Unbeknownst to the agents of the Architects, the Jammers intercepted this crucial message. They used their contacts in the Netherworld to figure out exactly what the key is. Unfortunately, the Jammers lack the resources to respond to this crisis immediately. Nor can they wait for reinforcements; by then it would be too late. What the Jammers need is a group to go into 2056 and recover the key for them. Can you see where this is going?

GETTING STARTED

This adventure starts best if the characters are already in the Netherworld. Ideally, they should be returning from a successful mission when they get hooked into this one. It's also best for characters who have some understanding of the secret war. They won't be too concerned about the threat of the Architects of the Flesh if they don't even know who the Architects are. Note that the characters don't have to actually have been to the future, they just need to know about it. If they are already working for the Prof, so much the better.

As for the reason that the Jammers pick the PCs to be their stooges, this is left up to the individual GM. Maybe the PCs have already made a name for themselves. Maybe they are enemies of the Jammers, who hope to solve two problems with one explosion. Or maybe they just happened to be at the right place at the right time.

The Plan: An ex-Buro scientist, Jammer, and dweller in the Netherworld named **Jack Footen** is the point man for this mission. He has to recruit the PCs and get them on the move. He's already used the Jammers' portal generator to create a gate from the Netherworld to the town in 2056 near the strip mine. That's the group's first stop—to visit the strip mine, pose as Buro agents, and retrieve the key. From there, he'll lead the PCs through another portal (guarded by the Lotus) to modern-day Lantau island near Hong Kong. There the group must reach the feng shui site and gain entrance. Footen will then try to destroy the site while the PCs are busy dealing with Pai Lai—whom, of course, Footen has not bothered to warn the PCs about.

OPENING SCENE

While wandering through the seemingly-endless passages of the Netherworld, the PCs are approached by a manic-looking individual. He is dressed in a drab gray lab coat of some unspecifiable material. He is breathing heavily and has a desperate look to him. When he sees the PCs, a look of relief passes over his face. Any PC who has spent time in the Netherworld and makes a Mind check can recognize the guy as Jack Footen, one of the Netherworld rabble and a former worker at the Buro's factory in the Netherworld. Ideally, the PCs should have already met him at Club Genocide or someplace else earlier in your campaign. As far as the PCs know, he isn't allied to any faction in the secret war—he's just one of the many people who have gotten caught in the turmoil and are making the best of things. (In fact, he's a Jammer—but so far he's kept that affiliation secret.) He approaches the PCs and, after pausing to pull himself together, addresses them.

Footen needs the PCs' help. He explains (if the PCs don't already know) that he used to work for the Buro but left when he grew disillusioned with the Buro's operations. He's been living in the Netherworld ever since, as 2056 is too dangerous for him to stay in.

Footen says he's been keeping tabs on his former employers, and particularly on his old boss, a Buro scientist named **Dr. Matthew Hunter** who screwed him over and was most responsible for driving him out of the Buro and his home juncture. Footen says he's been monitoring Hunter's transmissions to the Buro, and just learned something important.

At one of the Buro's massive strip mines in the 2056 juncture (specifically, in what used to be China), diggers found an odd item locked within a stone vault. It's a magical artifact of some sort. The Buro doesn't know what it is, but Footen does: a key created by a sorceror in ancient China that allows access to a powerful feng shui site. Footen knows Dr. Hunter has been called in to check out the key, and Footen doesn't want the Buro—and especially his nemesis, Dr. Hunter—to benefit from the key or the site.

He begs the PCs to help him. Time is of the essence, since he just intercepted the transmission and knows that the key will be retrieved shortly. Footen knows of a little-used gate from the Netherworld that'll take them to a town near the strip mine, and from there they can travel to the mine and retrieve the key. Then the feng shui site will be theirs.

No doubt the PCs will have some questions for Jack Footen. His responses to the most likely questions are provided below. *Don't spit out these answers verbatim;* paraphrase them in your own words or work elements of them into the general conversation to get the point across. It's important that the PCs trust Footen, at least partially, and if you begin reading text straight from this book when they ask him questions it's bound to make the players more suspicious.

What's in it for us? "I don't care about Feng Shui sites, I only want revenge on Dr. Hunter and the Buro. If you help me, I'll take you to the Feng Shui site in 1996 and you can control it."

How did you end up in the Netherworld? "I worked here for the Buro in their Netherworld-Arcanowave factory. When I got sick of their system, this was the only place I had a chance of making it in. Had I stayed in 2056, I'd be dead meat."

Why did you approach us? "I didn't want to hand over a good feng shui site to one of the other major factions. And from what I've heard, you're not just interested in power." This answer may need to be modified depending on the particular history of your group.

Where is the key now? "The key was unearthed at a strip mine and it's still there now. We have to get it before the science team led by Hunter shows up."

Why was this feng shui site locked up? "That I don't know and it has been puzzling me."

Can we go get equipment/go talk to the Prof, etc.? "No, we must leave immediately. Time is short."

Are you a Jammer? "No, certainly not. Those barbarians have no idea what forces they are messing with. I was an arcanowave scientist, and I know—blowing up feng shui sites is not only irresponsible, it's downright dangerous."

Footen should seem like a man driven over the edge by the autocratic future. It is vital that he appear honest and his story convincing. The adventure rides on it, so play up his slightly-crazed nature. He should seem eccentric but not dangerous. If the PCs have magic abilities that could reveal Footen's intent, do your best to camoflauge the results; much of what Footen says is true, and many of his stated goals are also true. He's not lying (in most things) so much as leaving out the truth.

Jack Footen

Once a loyal Buro scientist working on arcanowave technology, Footen lost big on inter-departmental politics and saw his boss, Dr. Matthew Hunter, take credit for his best work. Footen disappeared into the Netherworld, and was soon approached by other 2056 expatriates—who were also Jammers. Irrational and vindictive, Footen signed on with the Jammers to get revenge against the Buro. (It didn't hurt that the Jammers are also irrational and vindictive.) He doesn't care that much about the Jammers' plan to remove chi from human affairs; he thinks that goal is laughable. But anything that makes the Buro hurt is fine by him, and he's very loyal to Battlechimp Potemkin and the rest of the Jammers. Now that he has the chance to hurt Dr. Hunter personally, he's doubly eager and doubly irrational. Play him as a crazed scientist with a vendetta, but keep in mind that Footen is quite intelligent and that some portion of his crazed scientist role is a ruse; how much is real and how much isn't is something that not even Footen is sure of.

Jack Footen
Sample Dialogue: "Soon I'll make them all pay. They'll rue the day they messed with Jack Footen!"
Attributes: Body 5, Chi 3 (Magic 7), Mind 7, Reflexes 6
Skills: Arcanowave Devices 12, Deceit 14, Driving 12, Fix-it 14, Guns 11, Info/Secret War 12, Medicine 10, Sabotage 12
Weapons: Buro 9 (10/1/17+1), Buro Backup Arm (8/1/5+1)
Arcanowave Schticks: Twister Bullets, Wave Scanner

GETTING TO THE PORTAL

Footen will lead the PCs through the unearthly tunnels of the Netherworld. While other people are occasionally seen, Footen seems to go out of his way to avoid encountering anyone. The dimly-lit passages seem to go on forever, but Footen seems to know where he's going. Footen carries a big suitcase; says there are Buro uniforms inside that he stole from his old job. The PCs can change once they go through the gate, unless they feel like doing it now—but wandering around the Jammer-infested Netherworld in Buro uniforms isn't necessarily the best idea.

Soon, the group will come to a small side passage that leads nowhere. At the end of the passage, there is a small black void. This is the gate to 2056 that will lead them out near the strip mine.

SCENE 1: PRIDE 138

The PCs emerge into a dark room. After a bit of fumbling, Footen gets a dim lamp working. The room looks like a concrete cell. There is one narrow bed and one green plastic chair that are both labeled with stickers that read "Property of Transients' Slumber Facility #13." There is a window to the street, but it is currently shuttered.

Footen says they're in the backwater town of Pride 138, near the strip mine. He looks out the window and curses. It's already an hour past dawn, he explains, and Hunter's team will be here soon. He opens the big suitcase and the PCs see that it's filled with clothes. They are all gray and have different emblems on them. No matter how large the party, Footen will have enough uniforms for everyone. If the group contains any Abominations, they can be disguised as bodyguards. This will actually lend credence to their story, since only important scientists rank Abomination bodyguards.

While they're changing, the PCs hear the howl of sirens. Two sleek black cars pull up outside the window. Eight PubOrd officers with shotguns jump out of the cars, ready for action. Unless the PCs jump the gun, the PubOrd officers will smash open the door of the building across the street and rush inside. There's a brief struggle inside, along with the sounds of doors slamming, dishes flying, etc. A few moments later, a woman is dragged out of the building in her bedclothes. She looks to be in shock.

Footen will caution them to stay out of it. If any of the PCs actually go down to the street, however, they hear a PubOrd officer reading the near-catatonic woman the charges: "You and your husband are charged with disturbing the peace, assault on a PubOrd officer, and suspicion of anti-social thinking." If the PCs keep watching, they will see the PubOrd officers shove the woman into a car.

As the PubOrd cars pull away, the PCs hear the sound of stomping feet. Marching up the street is a column of school children in identical uniforms. As they march up the street, children emerge from the apartment blocks and join the procession. As they march, they chant, "We are 138! We are 138! We are 138!" Footen explains that the children are on their way to school.

If anyone asks about the origin of Pride 138's name, Footen tells them it's a product of one of the Buro's less-successful campaigns. The Buro sought to increase civic pride by naming new towns in rural areas Pride; needless to say, by the time they hit the 138th town named Pride, the campaign lost its novelty.

TO THE STRIP MINE

After the school children march off, it's finally quiet on the street. Footen indicates that it's safe to leave and mumbles under his breath about "infernal delays." He leads them to an elevator, which takes them to a parking garage under the Transients' Slumber Facility. He has a big white van painted with symbols that match those on the uniforms the PCs are now wearing. The group needs to get into the van and get it started. Footen, obviously, doesn't have a key. A PC (or Footen) needs to make a Fix-It check with a difficulty of 10. Footen can make this automatically if no PC can do it.

Footen takes the wheel. He drives slowly through the streets of Pride 138 and the PCs can catch a good glimpse of the future. Pride 138 is singularly depressing. It consists of block upon block of identical gray buildings. Functional signs identify places with catchy names like "House of Yum Yum Food #23" and "Friendly Buddy BuroBank, Branch 138/4." The streets are practically empty except for PubOrd vehicles.

Eventually, Footen leaves the town behind and heads out into the country. After a few miles, it becomes clear that there is no agriculture in this region. The landscape is windswept and desolate. There seem to be mountains to the west, as well as a great hanging cloud of dust. Footen points at it and says, "That's where the mine is."

SCENE 2: THE STRIP MINE

The last mile of the drive is uphill. When the slope levels off, the PCs can finally see the strip mine. Stretching out before them is the largest strip mine they've ever seen. It has a diameter of at least two miles. There are ten levels and the center is about a half-mile down. Dozens upon dozens of machines—crawling with workers—are at work digging, transporting, and sorting. The air is thick with dust and debris and all the workmen wear masks of some kind. Many also wear ear protection, as the noise is deafening. A fence encloses the entire facility and there is a small compound of buildings to the left of the road that overlooks the mine.

Two men flag down the van as it approaches. Footen says, "Leave this to me," and pulls over. The men wear grimy PubOrd uniforms and seem rather lethargic. "Good day, Consumer. What is your business at Buro Mining Facility 615?" Footen answers, "We're here to see Chief Engineer Marlowe. I believe he is expecting us. We're Dr. Hunter's team." Footen flashes his ID, which the guard barely glances at. He steps away from the van and starts yelling into a small phone. After a few moments of "What? What!", the guard returns and says, "Marlowe is in Sector 49. Just follow the signs."

Sector 49: Footen drives into the mine and starts trying to navigate. It takes about five minutes to make it down to Sector 49. Trucks and bulldozers are hard at work in this sector, as are some of the automated digging machines that do the actual mining. Footen drives up to a small building and stops. He turns and says, "OK, who wants to be Dr. Hunter? Don't worry, we're just here to pick up the artifact. Just act like you're in charge and he'll buy it." Presumably, some PC takes on the role. Footen has no ID to back it up; the PC just has to be loud and overbearing enough to get his way.

As the PCs get out of the van, a middle-aged man in a hardhat approaches. He identifies himself as Marlowe and asks which one is Dr. Hunter. Marlowe is a hard-working man who lacks much imagination. He just wants to hand over the artifact and be done with it. As long as the PCs don't do something stupid, he'll buy their story. He apologizes for their having driven down here; the item is back up in the compound.

At this point, Marlowe's phone rings. He steps away and answers it. After much yelling and confusion, he comes back. "I've got a problem down in Sector 65 that I need to take care of now. If you'll just drive back to compound, I'll meet you there as soon as I can."

Marlowe is lying. The phone call was from the real science team, who are approaching the mine with a heavy escort. Unless the PCs take drastic action now, Marlowe will drive off further down the mine and leave them to find their way back up to the compound. He knows the science team is going to come in with guns blazing, and he wants to get clear.

ON LOCATION

The road back up to the compound from Sector 49 has no turn-offs or stops, though it is wide enough for two vehicles to pass or for one to turn around. Sector 49 opens up onto a small plateau of sorts, with a checkpoint and ramps down to where heavy equpment is operating in this sector. The PCs will be wanting to go back up to the compound when trouble starts. It's up to the GM to decide whether the attack comes while the PCs are at the checkpoint in Sector 49, on the road back up to the compound, or in the compound itself. Since the science team is pretty well-equipped, the GM should stage the battle at or near the compound if the PCs are few in number or are not very experienced. If the PCs are mondo action heroes, have the attack come while the PCs are still at Sector 49, so they have to fight their way back up to the compound. Assuming that some portion of the battle takes place back up topside, here's some info on the compound.

There are three buildings in the compound: a cafeteria, a guardhouse, and the mine HQ.

Building 1, the Cafeteria: This large (30'x60') building is where the mine workers eat and spend their breaks. It is made of aluminum and was not built to last. It's full of wooden tables and chairs and also contains a large kitchen. At this time of day, there is no one here but the kitchen staff, and they will certainly flee when things start blowing up.

Building 2, the Guardhouse: This 20'x20' concrete building is where the night guards spend most of their time. There is a desk and a cot inside, as well as a locked wall case with three shotguns in it. When the shooting starts, there are two PubOrd officers here having a late breakfast. They've just gotten off night shift and are not in the mood for a fight. They'll stay out of the combat unless someone comes into the building or unless the PCs need someone else to beat up on.

Building 3, the Mine HQ: This 30'x40' building is also made of concrete. There are only two rooms inside. The front room is the communications center of the mine. There are three desks in here belonging to mine functionaries and a bank of phones and computers. The back room is Marlowe's office. It has a desk, a file cabinet, and bookshelves. He also has his own computer and his desk is covered with printouts.

The key is in his upper desk drawer. The key is a small golden box inscribed with magical characters. It can be carried easily in one hand. Closer inspection shows that the box is latched shut and can be opened. Inside the box is what appears to be a miniature human head. If touched, the skin proves to be quite

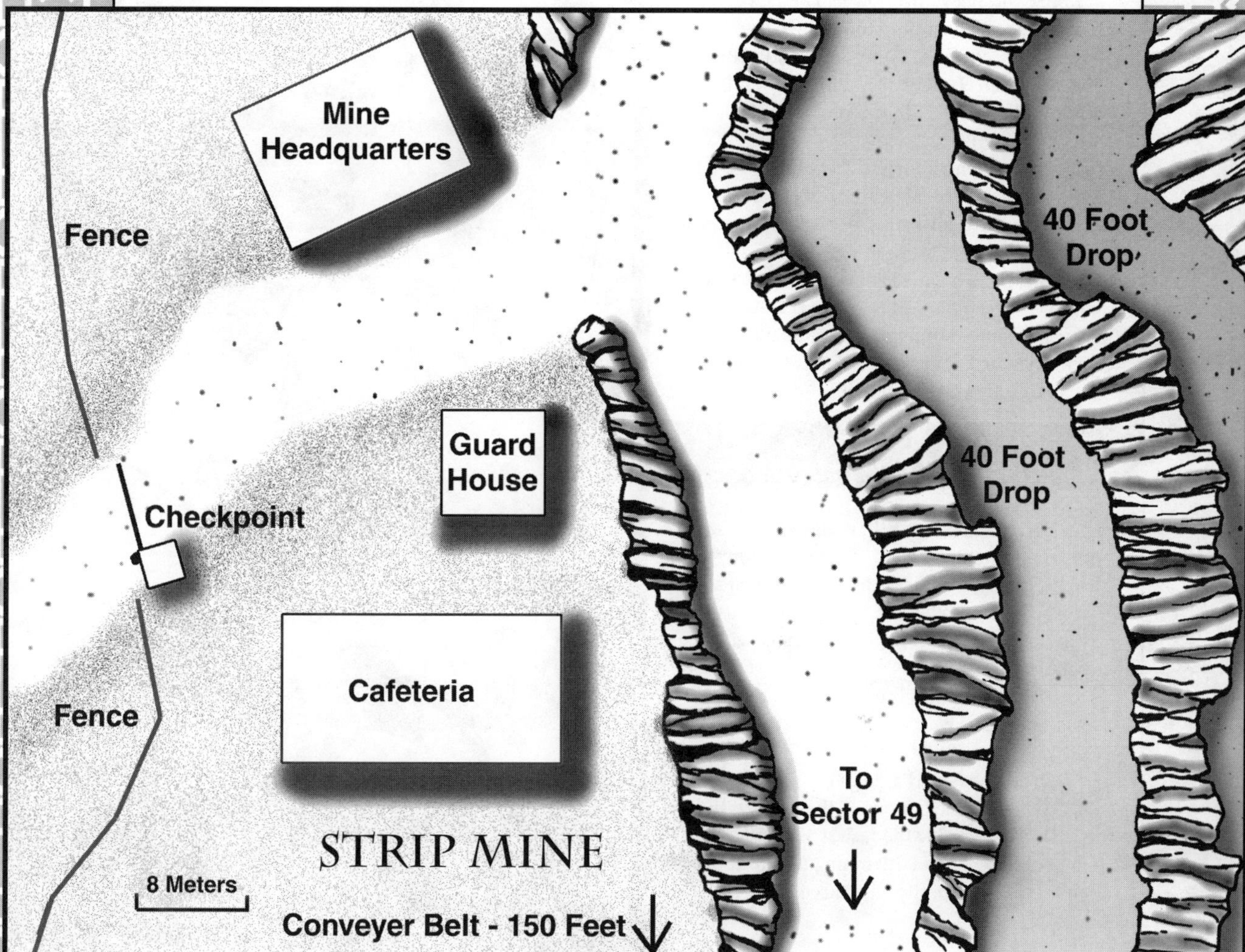

lifelike. Perceptive PCs may also notice the head's eyes darting back and forth.

ABOMINATION AMBUSH

The real science team is approaching the strip mine in helicopters. The PCs will see them coming if they are keeping a lookout. Otherwise, there is just too much noise to hear them coming. If they don't see the helicopters, the PCs will only become aware of them when a missile explodes near the van and almost rocks it over. Then they will see three black helicopters flying over the rim of the strip mine. It's time for a firefight!

Of the three helicopters, only one is an attack helicopter. The other two are transports. One is full of Abominations and the other has the actual science team and three human soldiers. The real Dr. Hunter and two assistants will head directly towards the compound where the key is. The second transport will slow down and release a squad of unnamed flying Abominations on the PCs (the squad contains two Abominations per PC). Meanwhile, the attack helicopter will provide support and heavy firepower. The PCs basically have a race against time on their hands. They need to get up to the compound and get the key before Dr. Hunter flies off with it, all the while fighting off flying Abominations and an attack helicopter.

Jack Footen will try to stay out of the fight, although he's perfectly willing to drive. For combat driving, his manic personality is a positive boon, especially when dodging missiles. (Remember he has a Driving skill of 12.) He will try to keep the van in one piece. And if the PCs ever want to find the feng shui site, they had better make sure that Footen stays in one piece, too, to bring them there.

NEAT THINGS THAT COULD HAPPEN

- The strip mine is full of equipment that's just screaming to be used. There are dump trucks, bulldozers, giant drills, and steam shovels. The crews of these vehicles will flee as soon as the bullets start to fly, leaving them wide open for PC use.
- The mine is also littered with tools of all sorts, as well as blasting caps and boxes of explosives.
- Of major note is a large conveyer belt that takes ore from the bottom of the mine to the top. This is probably the fastest way out of the mine, although any PC running up the conveyer belt will make a pretty easy target.

GMC NOTES FOR THE STRIP MINE

Here are the combatants the PCs will be facing during this battle.

Unnamed Flying Abominations

These monstrosities used to be Ogres in ancient China. Now they look even worse—seven-foot horrors with bulging muscles, huge teeth, and armored implants. They don't say much, but they do kick ass.

Unnamed Flying Abomination
Sample Dialogue: "Raaaaaaa!"
Attributes: Body 12, Chi 0 (Magic 7), Mind 3 (Per 6), Reflexes 7
Skills: Arcanowave Devices 10, Creature Powers 10, Guns 10, Intimidation 9, Martial Arts 12
Schticks: [Arcanowave] Aerial Mobility Unit, Wave Scanner. One Abomination carries a Helix Ripper, another a Helix Rethreader, and a third a Tracer Resin Projector. [Creature] Armor x2 (4 points), Damage Immunity (immune to falling damage)
Weapons: Buro Godhammer (12/4/5), those without Arcanowave weapons have Buro Hellharrowers (14**/8/20)

Roscoe the Buro BR-97 Attack Helicopter

This big honking chopper essentially acts as a GMC combatant during the fight. It's state-of-the-art Buro goodness, and should be considered a named character in play unless your PCs are wimps. Being a named character doesn't mean the chopper is sentient or anything—it'd just be a shame if, like some loser unnamed combatant, it went down on the first shot. You can, however, allow the PCs to make called shots or other funky attacks that would affect the pilot, rather than trying to take down the chopper itself through brute force. Attacks on the back rotor or other sensitive parts of Roscoe could also work, though Roscoe's Toughness of 20 will stop most minor attacks. The pilot is a standard mook GMC, but he benefits from Roscoe's Toughness—in other words, he doesn't die until you're good and ready for him to die. Til then, let Roscoe beat up on the PCs and take some occasional damage itself (novel use of spells or other special abilities will probably save the PCs' bacon). And don't forget the van is good for some PC armor, too.

The BR-97 is a descendent of the famed AH-64 Apache, though it is considerably more reliable and, of course, has numerous technological innovations for superior piloting, target acquisition, and weapons systems. Roscoe doesn't have all the goodies that other BR-97s have, and in particular is lightly-armed (by modern Buro standards) for its present assignment—the Buro wasn't counting on a bunch of meddling innerwalkers—but it's still a big fat wad of trouble for the PCs.

Roscoe the Buro BK-97 Attack Helicopter
Sample Dialogue: *Whup whup whup BUDDA BUDDA BUDDA BUDDA whup whup whup*
Attributes: Body 10, Chi 0, Mind 0, Reflexes 6
Skills: Driving 14, Guns 9
Weapons: Buro Megathreat 30mm Caseless Chain Gun (15/—/1500), Buro Woodchuck 70mm Missiles (25/—/72)

Dr. Matthew Hunter

Dr. Hunter is a trusted Buro scientist. He is loyal if not particularly devious. Although he carries a big gun, he actually is a bit of a coward. He talks a good game and will certainly tell the PCs of the horrid retribution the Buro will inflict on them if they don't surrender. Then he resorts to posturing with his Buro Godhammer. If waving around his big gun doesn't scare off the PCs, he will most likely take a hit, go down, and then play dead.

Dr. Hunter's Assistants

These are two faceless Buro scientists. They'll follow Dr. Hunter's lead.

Dr. Mattew Hunter
Sample Dialogue: "Footen! You fool! You'll ruin your credit rating!"
Attributes: Body 5, Chi 1 (Magic 5), Mind 6, Reflexes 5
Skills: Arcanowave Devices 10, Fix-it 12, Guns 8, Info/Buro 12, Leadership 10
Arcanowave Schticks: Spirit Shield Generator (2 spirits left), Twister Bullets
Weapons: Buro Godhammer (12/4/5)

Hunter's Unnamed Assistants
Sample Dialogue: "Dr. Hunter, look out! Aagh!"
Attributes: Body 4, Chi 0 (Magic 3), Mind 5, Reflexes 5
Skills: Arcanowave Devices 8, Info/Science 8, Guns 8
Weapons: Buro Backup Arm (8/1/5+1)

Buro Soldiers

These three soldiers are attached to the science team. They'll die without complaint.

Unnamed Buro Soldiers
Sample Dialogue: "Stop—" *blam blam blam blam* "—or I'll shoot!"
Attributes: Body 6, Chi 0, Mind 4, Reflexes 6
Skills: Guns 9, Intimidation 8, Martial Arts 9
Weapons: Buro Crimestopper (13/5/7), Buro 9 (10/1/17+1), Dagger (9)

PubOrd Officers

These are the night watchmen. They are not enthused about having to fight after working all night.

Unnamed PubOrd Officiers
Sample Dialogue: "I'm gonna activate your insurance policy, Consumer!"
Attributes: Body 5, Chi 0, Mind 5, Reflexes 5
Skills: Guns 8, Intimidation 8, Martial Arts 8, Info/Mine 10
Weapons: Buro Crimestopper (13/5/7), Billyclub (8)

BACK TO THE NETHERWORLD

Having retreived the key, the PCs and Footen will speed back to Pride 138 and the Netherworld portal, either in the van or in a stolen vehicle from the compound. It only takes a few minutes to get back to town, but if the PCs have had an easy time of it, throw another Roscoe at them as they near Pride 138—or have a PubOrd squad in the streets, mobilizing to stop the group. If the PCs have been fighting tooth and nail, though, let them get back to town safely; Pride 138 is in the middle of nowhere, and the PCs have already dealt with the major combatants in the area. Returning to the building, the PCs and Footen plunge through the gate and are as safe as usual.

The PCs can take a little time to rest after their brush with the future. While everyone is resting, Footen is consulting some hand-written notes and mumbling to himself. When they are ready, Footen again leads them through the Netherworld. This time he is not quite so sure where he is going and the group doubles back more than once. If asked just where he is leading them, Footen replies, "We need to go to Lantau. And there should be a portal around here somewhere."

WHAT IF THEY FAILED?

If the PCs didn't retreive the key but still escaped, it's bad news. The Buro will soon learn what the key leads to, and claim the feng shui site for themselves. The PCs can stake out the site on Lantau in the hopes of stopping Dr. Hunter (or the Buro dork who takes his place if he's dead), but they can't be sure just when the Buro will show up. You should be generous and assume that the Buro shows up soon after the PCs do. The Buro will come expecting a fight, but since this isn't their home turf they'll send a handful of capable, named GMCs and a handful of mooks to take the site rather than a bunch of attack choppers and abominations. Play out the fight on Lantau as you wish, using the information in this text as a guideline. Either the PCs will defeat the Buro and get into the site alone, or the Buro will get into the site and the situation will devolve into a massive free-for-all between the PCs, the Buro, and Pai Lai.

SCENE 3: THE BRIDGE OF DEATH

As if on cue, the PCs come around a corner and into a large chamber. As they enter the chamber, a blare of trumpets breaks the silence—a magical warning that activates when someone nears the threshold. So much for surprise.

The chamber they have entered is large (about 100'x150') and roughly hewn. At the far end of the chamber is a small pagoda and an elaborate arch (this is the portal). In front of the pagoda is a moat that stretches the length of the chamber; it's about 40 feet across. A single wooden planked bridge swings over the moat (the kind you've seen a million times in adventure movies). The moat appears to be about 50 feet deep and has some nasty-looking rocks down below.

This portal is guarded by the Eaters of the Lotus. It leads to Lantau, which is near where the Lotus' most important agent in our time, **Kun Chau**, resides (see the Hong Kong chapter in the main rulebook). To keep the influence of other factions at a minimum in Lantau, Gao Zhang has stationed a small force at this portal to dissuade Netherworld travelers from using it. Leading this force is **Jiang Biao**, a eunuch sorcerer from 69 AD. He has the aid of **Cho Kui**, a demonic ally, and eight **Thorns of the Lotus** (Lotus mooks).

When the trumpets sound, Jiang Biao and his troops take up positions on the other side of the moat. The three Thorns with bows stay on the top floor of the pagoda and choose their targets. Jiang Biao walks out to the bridge surrounded by the rest of the Thorns. Cho Kui stays out of sight in the bottom floor of the pagoda.

Jiang Biao will address the PCs. "You cannot pass this way. This portal belongs to the Eaters of the Lotus. Depart now or face the consequences."

The PCs can try talking their way out of this but it's just no good. Jiang Biao is there to make sure only Lotus operatives use this portal and that's exactly what he's going to do. When trouble starts, Jiang will start blasting. Cho Kui will stay hidden until he can maximize the element of surprise.

When the PCs get onto the bridge, they will see why it is called the bridge of death. The first sequence anyone is on the bridge, the stones below sprout razor-sharp spikes. In the second sequence, the spikes begin to shoot upwards at anyone on the bridge (one spike per attack, AV 8, Damage 6, Speed 2). In the third sequence, the bottom of the moat erupts with roaring flames. The spikes continue to fly up, only now they are white hot (Damage 8). Anyone who falls into the moat at this point has one sequence of falling time before they hit bottom. If they're an unnamed character, they are impaled, smashed, and incinerated all at the same time. If they can't be saved or save themselves in that one sequence, don't bother to roll damage. They're dead. If they're a named character (such as a PC), they land on a safe spot within the moat but are surrounded by flaming spikes and other horrible bits. Due to the intense heat and searing flame of the moat, they'll take 4 wound points for the first sequence they're there, then 8 the second sequence, then 12, and so on. They'll need help to get out of the moat, unless they have flying abilities of their own. If no help is coming, the demon Cho Kui can rescue the hapless PC—in order to deliver him to greater tortures of some other sort, of course! Demons don't do favors.

NEAT THINGS THAT COULD HAPPEN

- Cho Kui could fly out of the pagoda and try to knock PCs off the bridge.
- It is possible to cross the moat by climbing the walls on the sides of the chamber. If anyone tries to do that, Jiang Biao will try to blast them off the wall if he's free.
- Dying mooks could try to pull PCs into the moat with them (or vice versa).
- The old cut-the-ropes-of-the-bridge routine. (The Lotus can always re-shape another bridge!)
- At least one mook has to fall into the flaming spiky moat so the PCs can appreciate the fate they narrowly avoided.
- The pagoda can also be lit on fire… or just blown up.

GMC NOTES

Here are the bad guys at the Lotus gate.

Jiang Biao

Jiang Biao is a eunuch sorcerer of the Eaters of the Lotus. He was given the job of defending this portal by Gao Zhang himself and he means to keep it safe. Jiang has high hopes of rising through the ranks of the Eaters of the Lotus, therefore he doesn't want to die. If his situation looks hopeless, he will certainly flee. His humiliation would be great, however, and no doubt he would pursue any opportunity to avenge himself on the PCs.

THE BRIDGE OF DEATH

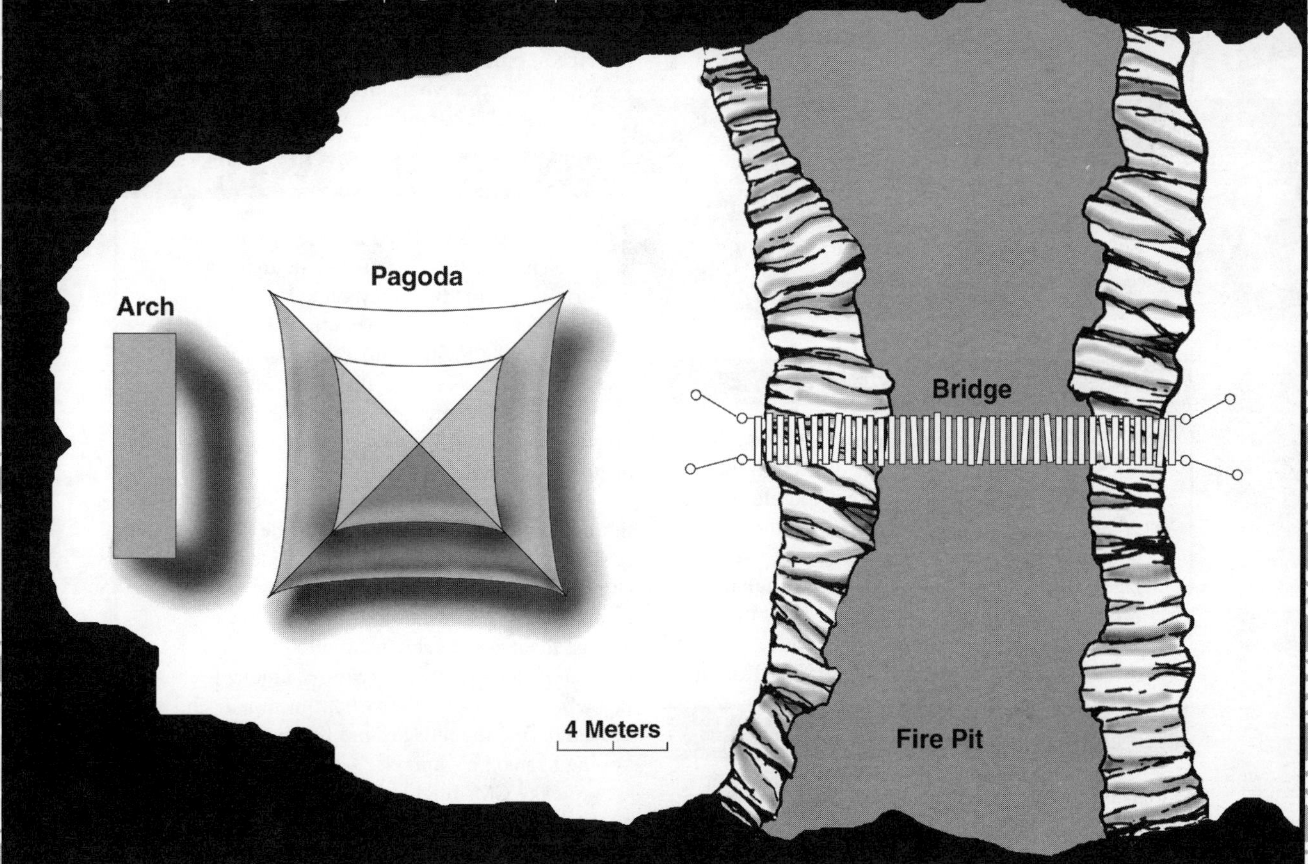

Jiang Biao
Sample Dialogue: "You will feel the wrath of the Lotus, upstart!"
Attributes: Body 6, Chi 3 (Magic 10), Mind 7, Reflexes 7
Skills: Guts 10, Leadership 14, Martial Arts 11, Sorcery 17, Stunts 15
Magic Schticks: Blast (base damage 12), Heal, Movement, Summoning
Weapon: Sword (10)

Cho Kui

Cho Kui is a demon bound in Jiang's service. Although he is small for a demon, he is more powerful than many lesser demons. His scaly skin is a vivid blue, rather unusually for a creature from the Underworld. Spiky protrusions cover his hands and tail; a green goo drips from his claws. Those who take too much of this goo into their bloodstreams become demons themselves (with the Corruption schtick). Jiang hopes to gain more minions this way. Cho Kui also has wings and is an expert at negotiating in caves.

Cho Kui
Sample Dialogue: "Yes, master. Of course I'm loyal to you, master."
Attributes: Body 9, Chi 4 (Magic 8), Mind 6, Reflexes 6
Skills: Creature Powers 10, Intimidation 12, Martial Arts 14
Creature Schticks: Abysmal Spines x2, Armor x 3 (6 points), Conditional Escalation (gains 1 body when target of Fu power), Corruption, Damage Immunity (immune to normal bullets), Flight.
Weapons: Claws and tail (14)

Thorns of the Lotus

The Thorns are Lotus mooks. They are fanatical soldiers loyal to Gao Zhang. They'll happily die for him. Good thing, too.

Thorns of the Lotus
Sample Dialogue: "You'll never defeat us!"
Attributes: Body 6, Chi 1, Mind 4, Reflexes 6
Skills: Intimidation 8, Martial Arts 8
Weapons: Three have bows (7/5/1) and daggers (9). The rest have spears (10).

THE PORTAL

When Jiang Biao and his thugs have been dealt with, the PCs will be free to pass through the portal. This portal looks like an elaborate arch of red and gold draped with black banners. The banners sing the praises of Gao Zhang, the Eaters of the Lotus, and the Emperor, in that order. While it doesn't actually look like the arch leads anywhere, anyone who passes through it will end up in contemporary Lantau.

SCENE 4: LANTAU

The rest of the adventure takes place on the island of Lantau. Lantau is a large island to the west of Hong Kong. Although it is almost twice as large as Hong Kong, it has a population of less than 10,000 (compared to HK's population of over a million). This is largely due to the fact that Lantau is extremely mountainous (in fact Lantau is also known as Tai Yue Shan or Big Island Mountain). In addition to a number of fishing communities, Lantau is also home to some important monasteries, most notably the Trappist Haven Monastery and the Buddhist Po Lin Monastery.

The PCs come through the portal into a back alley in the town of Mui Wo, called Silvermine Bay by Westerners. Mui Wo is on the east coast of Lantau and it's where all the ferries from Hong Kong dock. Almost a third of Lantau's population lives here and the tourist trade keeps them quite busy. It's possible to get buses to all other parts of the island here.

The PCs arrive in the mid-afternoon. No one notices their appearance in the alley. The alley itself smells awful and appears to be behind a seafood restaurant. It's full of garbage bins and smells heavily of rotting fish. If they haven't already, now would be a good time to ditch their 2056 duds.

Disappointingly, there is just nothing sinister in this town. Footen tells the PCs that they need to catch a bus to the Po Lin Monastery because the feng shui site is near there. Anyone from contemporary HK knows about the Po Lin Monastery. It's a popular tourist spot that could well be called the Disneyland of Buddhism. The PCs will be thrilled to learn that they can check out the largest outdoor Buddha statue in the world, which stands a whopping 34 meters high and cost HK $20 million. Yowza.

PO LIN MONASTERY

Catching a bus up to Po Lin Monastery is no problem. The buses are frequent and comfortable. By the time they get to the monastery, it is late afternoon. If the PCs want to spend a night recuperating, they can get rooms at the monastery. If they don't, skip to the "Lantau Peak" section and assume the PCs arrive at Lantau Peak around sunset after a hike of just a couple hours.

The monastery is packed with tourists but there are a few rooms available for the PCs at a reasonable price. Dinner is also provided. Guests get to eat what the monks eat, which means purely vegetarian food. In fact, it is against the rules to bring meat into the monastery. Supernatural Creatures among the PCs who can't bear to be without meat may end up wandering the hills around the monastery hoping to snarf a squirrel.

Sneaky GMs might consider having some of the monks at the monastery be sensitive to Supernatural Creatures, Sorcerers, and other funky PC types. If so, the monks may ambush the relevant PCs to find out what they want (the monks don't know about the secret war, but are certainly well-versed in Chinese mysticism and the like) or just kick them out for being suspicious.

THOSE ANNOYING CAMPBELLS

Since the PCs haven't gone straight to Lantau Peak and are spending a night relaxing with the tourists instead of waging the secret war, they of course deserve to have a little misery thrown their way (not to mention a little comic relief). Introduce them to **the Campbells**.

The Campbells are an American family in Hong Kong on vacation. They are your basic white trash family bringing money and misery to the far east. **Henry**, the man of the house, used to work as a mechanic until he won the lottery two years ago. Now he lives high on the hog and wears only the best in Hawaiian shirts. His wife is named **Peggy**, although Henry often calls her Leggy instead. Henry and Peggy have graced the world with two terrors, **Mitch** (age 12) and **Suzy** (age 10). Both kids are spoiled rotten.

The Campbells will inflict themselves on the PCs at dinner, either because some of the PCs are westerners or just because they like the PCs' looks. Try to give everyone at dinner a taste of the Campbells and, of course, play the scene for laughs. Here are some suggestions for terrorizing your players with the Campbells.

- Henry will say things like, "Hey, what's with all these side dishes? Where's the meat? This stuff may be all right for you rice eaters, but I'm an American, by God. Where's my meat?" Or, "I hear the commies are taking over here in '97. That's too bad, but I hope none of these people come to America to take jobs away from hard-working folks like me. Right, Leggy?"
- Peggy is a bit more diplomatic. "Oh, don't mind Henry. He didn't want to come to Hong Kong but he promised to take me here years ago when I read about it in a travel magazine. It just seemed so romantic. And just imagine, people have lived here for thousands of years. Isn't that amazing..."
- Mitch is 12. This means lots of throwing stuff around and plenty of fart jokes. He also is unhappy about being in HK. "This sucks. Why couldn't we go to Disneyworld again? Can I get a cheeseburger here? Why are there so many statues of fat guys here?"
- Suzy is quieter than Mitch but no less annoying. Everything must be *just so.* "Did Dad tell you that I'm a princess? It's true, really. I command you to cut up my food! Hey what's that bulge in your jacket? I order you to show me!"

Keep this up until your players are begging you to let them kill the Campbells. Point out that many people get up before dawn so they can climb Lantau Peak by sunrise. By this point, four hours of sleep followed by a long hike may seem like an appealing option.

LANTAU PEAK

Lantau Peak is the second-highest peak in Hong Kong, standing at 933 meters. It is also the location of the feng shui site. It's about a 2 km walk to the peak. The PCs can pick up the Lantau Trail, a footpath that runs the length of the island and leads directly to Lantau Peak. Near the top of Lantau Peak, there is a small side path labeled "scenic overlook." Footen indicates that the site is up this small path.

Apparently, this path isn't used very often, since it is narrow and rather steep in places. The path ends about 50 meters from the peak. There is a natural alcove in the side of the mountain. This small area is littered with beer cans and fast food wrappers, a legacy of rowdy teens and tourists. In the back of the alcove there is an unnaturally-precise hole at eye level that's about one foot square. This little box is the "lock" the key opens.

Simply putting the gold box into the hole will not work. The PCs must take the miniature head out of the box and put it into the lock. When they do this, the head will start to grow. After a moment or so, the head will have grown to normal human size and the PCs will notice now (if they hadn't before) that the head is quite alive. It's eyes dart back and forth and then its mouth opens. Incredibly, it speaks. It's hard to understand what the head is saying but it seems to be some sort of incantation. As the seconds tick by, the incantation gets louder and faster. The head's face starts to contort and sweat and there is a rumbling in the mountain. The rocks in the alcove begin to vibrate and the stone seems like it's cracking. Footen will shout, "Get back!" and lunge down the trail. Smart PCs will follow him. Seconds later, the head's incantation will crescendo in a horrifying scream and the walls of the alcove will explode outward with terrific force, leaving a gaping hole in the side of Lantau Peak. The head is nowhere to be seen.

PAI LAI

After the explosion, the PCs will be able to enter the feng shui site. Most of the rock seems to have been blown out and down the mountain. Inside there is a large cave, dimly lit by a bluish light. The first thing the PCs will notice is that the cave is really cold. As they clamber over the fallen rocks, they'll see why. The floor is covered with ice, huge icicles hang from the ceiling, and even the walls have been covered with sheets of ice that reflect like mirrors. In the center of the room is a miniature replica of the Emperor's Palace that stands about five feet high and twenty feet long. In front of it is an army made of finely sculpted ice warriors at least 50 strong. These soldier statues are about a foot high and wear the ceremonial armor of the Emperor's guards. Behind the palace is another enormous sculpture. This one is almost twelve feet tall and almost as wide. It is the bust of an elderly Chinese man whose face is twisted by a sinister sneer. For those that might know, this is a depiction of Gao Zhang, leader of the Eaters of the Lotus.

As the PCs enter, a figure steps out from behind the ice Gao. It is clearly a demon. He stands over ten feet tall and has skin of jet black. He has a long serpent's head with glowing blue eyes and a tail to match. Four arms jut out from his heavily muscled torso, two ending in wicked blades and the other two with clawed hands. Although frost flecks his lips, he wears a blue robe loosely about him. If the PCs immediately attack, skip to the "Whacking on Pai Lai" section.

He stands next to the ice sculpture, patting it fondly, and addresses the PCs. "Gao Zhang said I never gave him face. Do you think this counts?" He starts laughing maniacally at his own joke. Finally, he'll calm himself. "So, has Gao sent you to kill me at last or have you come to join my legion?" He gestures at the little army of ice warriors in front of the miniature palace.

This demon, of course, is **Pai Lai** and he's quite mad. Almost two thousand years alone in a cave will do that to you. He's kept himself amused with his sculptures and his schemes of revenge, but eventually the solitude was too much for even a demon lord to bear. Now he is completely beyond reason. In his mind, either the PCs are there to bow down and worship him or they are there to kill him. Any other explanations simply don't make sense to him. He will listen for awhile and even seem to grasp what the PCs say, but eventually he'll blow up.

"I am Pai Lai, Demon Lord of the Six Agonies! You will grovel before me or perish horribly. Choose quickly!"

THE ICE CAVERN/TEMPLE

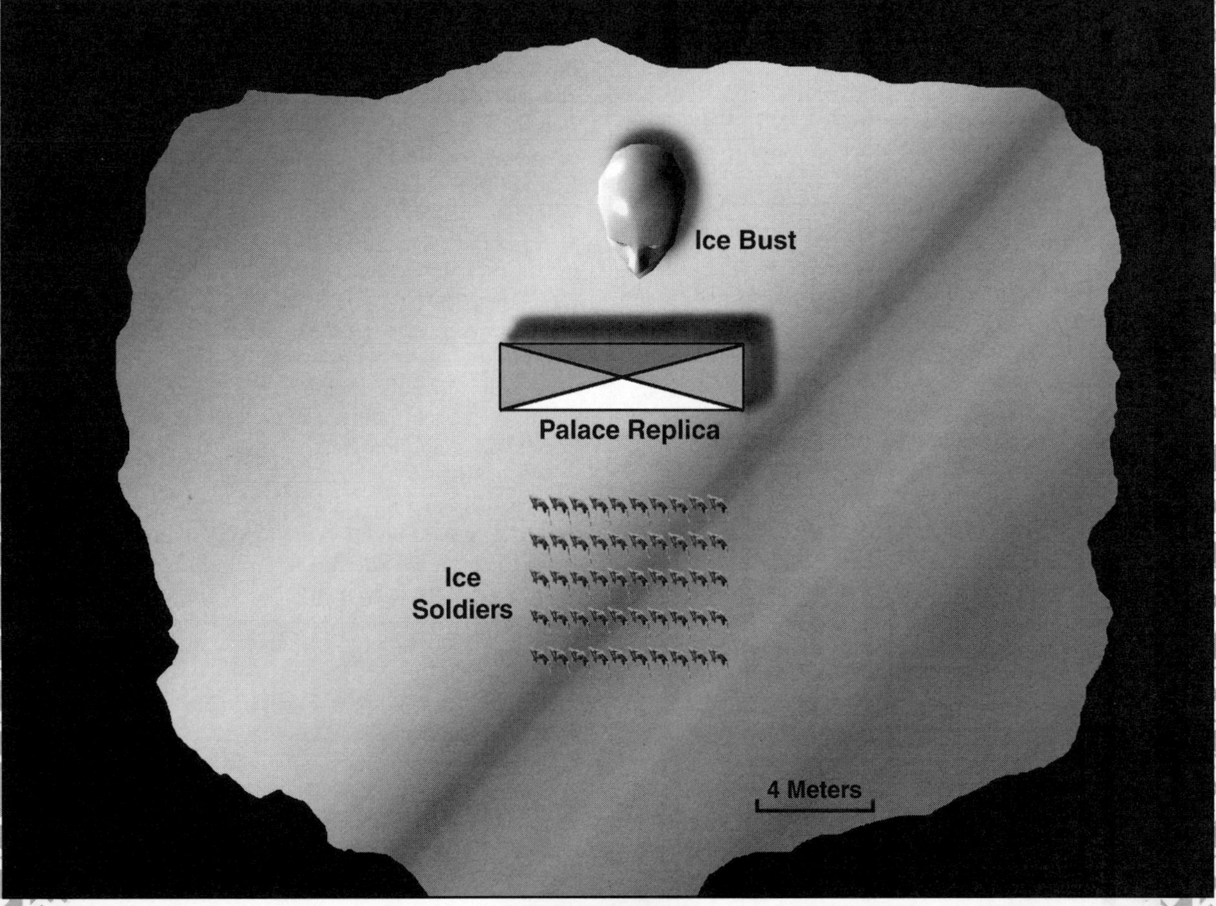

GMC NOTES

Here are the demon lord and his terrible creations, ready to rumble.

Pai Lai

Pai Lai used to be the Demon Lord of the Six Agonies. He lost his position and his special agony powers when he was imprisoned. Despite this, Pai Lai is quite powerful. Unfortunately, he's quite lost his mind. He has periods of lucidity but soon lapses into delusion. His story might even be tragic if he weren't a demon. I'm sure the PCs won't cry when they send him back to the Underworld.

Pai Lai
Sample Dialogue: "Which of the agonies would you like first? The betrayal of the one you love? Or perhaps something simple like being roasted alive?"
Attributes: Body 12, Chi 6 (Magic 10), Mind 6, Reflexes 8
Skills: Creature Powers 17, Deceit 12, Intimidation 12, Martial Arts 14, Sculpture 18
Creature Schticks: Abysmal Spines, Armor x2 (four points), Blast (when he touches his two bladed hands together, lightning shoots forth: base damage 12), Damage Immunity (immune to Fire Blasts), Regeneration x3, Soul Twist (base damage 13)
Weapons: Claws and tail (14)

Ice Soldiers

These are exquisite sculptures animated by Pai Lai's demonic power.

Ice Soldiers
Sample Dialogue: They're statues, they can't talk.
Attributes: Body 6, Chi 0 (Magic 5), Mind 2, Reflexes 5
Skills: Creature Powers 10, Martial Arts 10
Creature Schticks: Damage Immunity (immune to cold-based attacks and mental attacks).
Weapons: Naginata (10)

WHACKING ON PAI LAI

When the shooting starts, Pai Lai will duck behind the statue of Gao and say, "You have made your choice. Now face my legion!" As the PCs start to move, they'll notice that the soldier statues are beginning to grow quite rapidly. No doubt the PCs will start laying into them with all they've got. Let them wreak destruction on the statues as they grow, but in the end there will still be at least 10 of them left (more can be added to taste). Then it's a big brawl to the finish with a demon lord and his icy minions.

During the battle with Pai Lai, Jack Footen does his best to stay out of the way. He will hide behind an ice pillar for most of the battle. If any of the PCs goes down during the fight, however, he will drag them to safety and administer to their wounds. Besides this, though, Footen is busy—he's setting up a nasty bomb to take out the whole site. The PCs shouldn't clue in to this unless they specifically ask what Footen is doing—then they can realize that he isn't exactly being Mr. Helpful, but what he's doing is hard to say. Footen is off to one side, behind the pillars, fiddling with something.

NEAT THINGS THAT COULD HAPPEN

- There are some big icy pillars spread out across the room. These can be used for cover or for knocking on top of people.
- Pai Lai could roll the Gao bust at the PCs.
- Some of those icicles on the roof are big and pointy. If they were to fall on someone's head (say if they got shot off by a bolt of flame) that would really hurt.
- Someone really should slide across the icy ground with guns blazing.
- The craftsmanship on the miniature palace is exquisite. It really needs to be blown up! It can also be used as cover.
- A group of tourists show up at the cave. They've been drawn here by the explosion. Without thinking, they enter the cave and get caught in the firefight. Heroic PCs will try to save them, although it's also in keeping with HK movie sensibilities to let them get mauled by the bad guy. If you're feeling really mean, you can make this the Campbells, assuming the PCs met them.

FOOTEN'S SECRET

Assuming he isn't interrupted by the PCs, Footen will be busy setting up his nasty Jammer bomb to destroy the feng shui site. All he wants to do is set the bomb and get out—he doesn't particularly care what state the PCs, Pai Lai, or the ice soldiers are in when the bomb goes off. (However, if Footen has somehow become sympathetic to the PCs during the session, you may want to modify his actions accordingly.)

Just when the bomb goes off is entirely up to you. If it goes off while the PCs are in the site, they should be toast—so the key here is to tip off the PCs to what Footen is up to just in time for them to realize they have to deal with a big honking bomb as well as a big honking demon. The way to do this is to have someone notice Footen fiddling with some device off to the side, or else just running away from a curious-looking device on the floor and out the entrance to safety. Something like this should tip the PCs off that there's trouble, and if the PCs get a look at the device, they'll realize it's some weird sort of arcanowave explosive device that will go off Real Soon Now. Pai Lai, of course,

will have no idea what a "bomb" is and will not listen to frantic PC explanations of the terrible danger they're all in. He just wants to kill them.

One of several things is likely to happen:

Everyone goes boom. If the PCs don't stop the bomb or don't bother to leave soon enough, they and Pai Lai go up in a massive explosion and the players hate your guts. If this happens, it should only be because the players were simply not on the ball and ignored the hints you should have thrown in their face as the clock ticked.

Footen is stopped. The PCs can stop Footen either as he's mucking with the bomb or as he's running for the door. Either way, the bomb should already be alive and ticking. Footen admits he's a Jammer, and says it's too late to stop the bomb—it's a Battlechimp Potemkin special, and it can't be stopped. He calmly advises the PCs to leave the site and Pai Lai and let the bomb do its work.

The bomb is stopped. Footen is lying. Any PC can make an Arcanowave or Fix-It check (or any other check you deem appropriate) to deactivate the bomb. Defusing the bomb, however, has a Difficulty of 15. Botched rolls should shorten the amount of time remaining before the bomb goes off, unless you just want to snuff all the PCs for some reason. If one PC stays behind to stop the bomb while the rest run to safety, feel free to blow up that PC should a botch occur and cue the dramatic montage as her friends recall her brave sacrifice.

The bomb goes out the door. The PCs can grab the bomb and chuck it out the door. Assuming they make some reasonable rolls, the bomb goes off outside. Pai Lai, if he's still around, won't really care and will still want to wax the PCs. If you're feeling dramatic, have the explosion collapse the entrance, leaving the PCs temporarily trapped in the cave with the demon lord. Given time, the PCs (or outsiders) can clear the entrance—but for the moment, they have to rock and roll with Pai Lai.

ENDING THE FIGHT

When Pai Lai finally takes mortal wounds, he will fall to his knees. Breathing raggedly, he addresses the PCs one last time. "You have done what even Gao Zhang could not do. I am slain. But know this: when the icy hand of death reaches out for each of you, I will be there waiting. You cannot escape me."

He laughs one last time and this laugh turns into a roaring scream. Any remaining ice pillars and statues explode, as does the miniature imperial palace. The shock of the blast throws the PCs to the ground. Pai Lai's scream ends with his life and the PCs are left in the wreckage of his prison. Everyone is covered with ice.

WRAPPING UP

No doubt the heroic PCs will figure a way out of Footen's trap and foil the Jammers' plan. Well, maybe. When Footen is taken care of, Pai Lai is defeated, and the bomb situation is resolved, the adventure is over.

The PCs have some hard choices ahead of them. They can attune to the feng shui site but that has dangers as well as benefits. It may be that they simply don't have the resources to defend the site. If they do keep it, they'll have to figure out a way to keep tourists from wandering in off Lantau Trail. They may also have to deal with the authorities, especially if innocent bystanders got whacked in the final battle.

Looking back, the PCs have had the rare opportunity to make three sets of enemies in one shot, depending on how things went. The Lotus and the Architects will almost certainly want to take a piece out of the PCs' hide; the Jammers are probably off the PCs' best-buddy list for the time being, too. And just to make things interesting, if the site still exists then the Ascended's orbiting satellites might spot the resurgent feng shui site and if so, will almost certainly want to take it back. While the PCs may think they've just had a little bait-and-switch fiasco, in truth they've gotten themselves into big trouble with a lot of bad guys; many bad things are bound to ensue.

FURTHER ADVENTURES

- Gao Zhang will search intently for the people who attacked his minions in the Netherworld and killed Pai Lai. Gao is especially upset that Pai Lai has been "freed." He wanted the Demon Lord to spend the rest of eternity in that cave. So Gao Zhang will hunt for the PCs and try to exact his revenge. This is certainly the seed for a later adventure or series of adventures.
- The Architects of the Flesh were also slighted by the PCs. Film from surveillance cameras at the strip mine will certainly be sent to Buro labs for analysis. The PCs may be associated with the Jammers due to their alliance with Footen. That association could lead to trouble if the PCs ever cross into 2056 again.
- The PCs will probably end this story with a low opinion of the Jammers, and the feeling may be mutual if the PCs stopped the bomb.
- Finally, there is Pai Lai himself. It's possible that his dying curse was meaningless. It's possible that it was just words. Then again, villains have a nasty habit of coming back in *Feng Shui* and it could be that Pai Lai will one day return to seek his revenge on the PCs. Until then, let them live in fear

LUSIGNAN THE FOOL stomps about his chambers in the tower, dressed in full jester regalia. He paces around a large wooden chair, somewhat like a threadbare throne; an old human skull sits on the seat. He stops moving and begins to speak, quoting jumbled bits from *Hamlet*.

LUSIGNAN
(leaning, he taps the skull)
Not a mouse stirring.

(standing)
But in the gross and scope of my opinion, this bodes some strange eruption to our state.

(races to a window and bellows)
In the most high and palmy state of Rome, a little ere the mightiest Julius fell, the graves stood tenantless and the sheeted dead did squeak and gibber in the Roman streets!

(zips back to the skull and whispers)
But answer made it none. Give it an understanding, but no tongue.

(in a comical, ghostly voice)
I am thy father's spirit, doomed for a certain term to walk the night!

(in his own voice, patting the skull)
Rest, rest, perturbed spirit. By indirections find directions out.

(pacing, grandiloquent)
I have heard, that guilty creatures sitting at a play, have by the very cunning of the scene been struck so to the soul that presently they have proclaimed their malefactions; for murder, though it have no tongue, will speak with most miraculous organ.

(shaking his head)
I must be cruel only to be kind.

LUSIGNAN picks up the skull and sits down on the throne. He sets the skull in his lap, then leans forward and turns on a big old black-and-white television in front of him.

(perking up)
Hey, *Star Trek* is on!

JOHN TYNES

THE SHAPE OF GUILT

ILLUSTRATED BY HEATHER HUDSON

Premise: It's *Hamlet* meets *The Heroic Trio* when the ghost of the Four Monarchs' murdered father begins haunting the airwaves of IKTV and slandering his errant children.
The Twist: Everyone thinks that IKTV's owners are to blame. But it's really the Prof. No, actually it's Lusignan the Fool. No, actually it's the Monarchs themselves. No, it's really the dead father. Hey, what the heck is going on?
Climax: Huan Ken puts the Prof on trial, but the PCs have a surprise witness.

BACKSTORY

As described in the *Feng Shui* rulebook, the Four Monarchs murdered their father centuries ago when he refused to crown them as the rulers of the world. Since that time, the siblings have each become convinced that he or she participated unwillingly, and that the other three are really the ones to blame for the terrible event. In truth, they all did it willingly and with full knowledge of their actions—but when the guilt is too great, the mind revises history to be at ease with itself. And after all, it was such a long time ago. No one but the Monarchs knows about the murder of their father…

… except for **Lusignan the Fool**, once the court jester for **Huan Ken the Thunder King** and now a crazed troublemaker-at-large in the Netherworld. Like all fools, he knows more than he should and gets away with more than others could. Recently, he's decided to teach the Monarchs a lesson in humility.

Using magic and his shaping abilities, Lusignan is making use of the Monarchs' tremendous chi energy and their collective guilt over their father's murder to shape the broadcasts coming from **IKTV**, the idiosyncratic broadcasting outfit based in the Netherworld and run by **Columbia and Laurel Towson**. Lusignan set up a rebroadcasting link and infused it with magical energy, but what happens as a result is a manifestation of the Monarchs' self-hatred: the 'ghost' of their father appears sporadically on IKTV, railing against the Monarchs and hinting at his murder. He always knows just what to say to really hurt the siblings, since it's just their own projected self-hatred coming back at them. Needless to say, the Monarchs are mad as hell and they aren't going to take it anymore.

Enter the Prof: To pull off his scheme, Lusignan needed access to some high-tech goodies, and he also needed a place to hide his rebroadcast link. He chose the **Junkyard**, home of **the Prof**, and assembled his link (and the accompanying magical effects) there in secret. Not even the Prof knows it's there—but when she learns about it, she won't blab. Here's why.

Lusignan and the Prof: As noted in the rulebook, the Prof cannot leave the Netherworld owing to a curse placed upon her by Lusignan. That's pure bunk, a rumor the Prof has spread herself to cover up the truth. As always, the truth of the matter is stranger than the fiction.

Years ago, the Prof and Lusignan were lovers. The quirky pair got on well, but kept their relationship a secret. Eventually, Lusignan had to leave the Netherworld—but he also couldn't afford to let the Monarchs know he was gone. (Just where Lusignan went and what he's been up to since then are secrets that will not be revealed in this book; but they have no bearing on the story.) The Prof came up with the solution: she created a replacement Lusignan, a clockwork automaton given life and sentience through shaping and the magical abilities of Lusignan himself. The new Lusignan knows he is a fake, and is happy in his role. If anything, he's even more unstable and weird than the original. The reason why the Prof can't leave the Netherworld is simple: if she leaves the Netherworld, the magic that keeps the replacement Lusignan going will be broken and he'll collapse into a heap of parts. Without the real Lusignan, the Prof could not bring the parts back to life. So she's stuck in the Netherworld until the real McCoy returns. True to the Prof's nature, she doesn't see this as a big deal; she loves Lusignan, and will keep up the charade until he returns. But she also will not tell a soul about the fake Lusignan's secret, not even the PCs. Her refusal to turn against Lusignan during the course of this storyline will probably cause the PCs some serious trouble and confusion. Hey, that's love.

NOT YOUR FATHER'S SCENARIO

This is a sub-plot, not a stand-alone adventure. You can't just open the book to this page and start running *The Shape of Guilt* right out of the box, as it were. Instead, this is a plotline for you to work into your *Feng Shui* campaign. The text describes the major characters, the course of the storyline, specific events to work into your sessions, and ways for the PCs to be involved. For obvious reasons, your PCs will have to know enough about the secret war to be traveling through the Netherworld on a regular basis. It's also necessary that the PCs be on good terms with the Prof, if indeed they aren't actually working for her as the new Dragons. This requirement means you may have problems making use of this scenario, but look at it as an important goal: if the PCs develop enough of an attachment to a GMC to go to the wall for her, the players are probably pretty strongly engaged in the campaign and will welcome this opportunity to show their stuff.

This tale is presented in three acts, each with two suggested scenes. Each act spells out the major events and plot points for the act, as well as how to involve the PCs and what criteria you should or should not use the scenes by. Not every scene has to be used; it's up to you and the players.

Owing to this tale's peculiar structure and stringent requirements, plan ahead if you want to use it. By the time you activate this plotline, your campaign should be more than a loose string of scenarios; it should be an ongoing story, in which the major action is driven by PC goals rather than by whatever one-shot scenario you have at hand. Properly used, this storyline should work well and should reward players for their involvement in your campaign with an exciting story where the PCs are their own motivation.

GMC NOTES

Here are descriptions of the main GM characters in the story. Stats for the Four Monarchs are not provided; the PCs shouldn't have an opportunity to get into combat with them in this scenario, and the GM should just assume that the Monarchs can wax any normal PC within a sequence or two using whatever spells, weapons, or fu powers you care to pull out of your hat. Treat them more like gods than GMCs and you'll be on the right track. They *can* be defeated, but that's not going to happen this time around.

Lusignan the Fool, Enigmatic Jester

The quintessential court jester, Lusignan is a half-crazed (or else incredibly-cunning) guy who spent years in the service of Huan Ken the Thunder King's royal court. No one, not even Huan Ken, knows who Lusignan really is or where he came from. Some time ago, Lusignan's canny insults and open mockery grew too much for Huan Ken, who kicked him out. Since then, Lusignan has shaped himself a bizarre tower (see p. 231 of the rulebook) and has an uncanny knack for getting in the middle of sticky situations and making them stickier. He never seems to act out of outright malice, and he's generally considered to be a kindly guy with a barbed wit and a head full of beans. Still, he's always ticking off someone, and most DPs in the Netherworld assume that sooner or later he's going to end up dead. No one but Lusignan and the Prof know that the two are lovers.

As noted earlier, the real Lusignan left the Netherworld shortly after Huan Ken kicked him out of his court. His replacement—and the one most Netherworlders have met—is a clockwork automaton given magical sentience and life.

Lusignan the Fool
Sample Quote: "Oh, good sir, your influence is as great as the noonday sun, and just as enduring."
Distinguishing Features: Dresses like a jester. Hard to miss.
Attributes: Body 8, Chi 10 (Magic 14), Mind 10, Reflexes 6
Skills: Fix-It 10, Info/Four Monarchs 10, Info/Netherworld 12, Sorcery 18
Magic Schticks: Blast (base damage 16; special effects Fire, Ice, Steam), Heal, Movement, Weather

The Prof, Valiant Techie

Leader of the Dragons (which may or may not mean much of anything, depending on your campaign) and a quirky force for all that's good-hearted, the Prof is a wacky techie genius who never leaves the Netherworld. Within her home—known as the Junkyard (p. 231 in the rulebook)—she whips up all sorts of bizarro inventions and does what she can to save the world. Sometimes, it's a lot.

The Prof
Sample Quote: "Now where did I put that sonic shaper?"
Distinguishing Features: Frizzy white hair, lab coat, raucous laugh.
Attributes: Body 6, Chi 2 (For 7), Mind 10, Reflexes 5
Skills: Driving 15, Fix-It 20, Guns 11, Info/Netherworld 10, Info/Science 14

Columbia & Laurel Towson, Renegade Journalists

These twin sisters aren't a part of the secret war, really; they're just a couple of free-spirited independent operators. Unable to get good broadcasting jobs in the real world, they stumbled on the Netherworld and made it their home. Their pride and joy is IKTV (Inner Kingdom Television), a broadcasting station exclusively serving those in the Netherworld with television sets; Nielsen ratings data on their viewership is, understandably, non-existent. The sisters dislike the Monarchs, who remind them entirely too much of news directors and station managers back in the real world—in other words, authority figures. The Towsons are in their late twenties, and were both kicked out of the University of Missouri's prestigious journalism school on grounds of general flakiness. They have a strong bond, and like nothing better than to take apart their station's equipment and put it all back together again, "just in case something's wrong." Wirehead city. The sisters share identical stats.

Columbia & Laurel Towson
Sample Quote: "Stay tuned for the long-lost pilot episode of *Lost in Space!*"
Distinguishing Features: Short, slim, black hair, impossible to tell apart.
Attributes: Body 5, Chi 2 (For 5), Mind 7, Reflexes 6
Skills: Detective 10, Fix-It 6, Info/Broadcasting 12, Info/Netherworld Politics 10, Journalism 10, Martial Arts 5

Ming I, Queen of the Darkness Pagoda

Ming I's history is described on p. 203 of the rulebook. In the Netherworld, she is one of the four main powers (the other three being her siblings, of course) of the realm. Ambitious, intelligent, and a born schemer, Ming I still falls prey to her inflated self-importance quite often. Like all the Monarchs, Ming I is a tremendously powerful individual; her right arm is a magical limb of pure darkness with a variety of abilities. Within her Darkness Pagoda, a retinue of bloodthirsty and brooding priests engage in endless conspiracies against each other, to Ming I's delight.

Huan Ken, King of the Thunder Pagoda

Huan Ken is discussed on p. 204 of the rulebook. He's the most European of the Monarchs, having titled himself King and Pope and made his capital the Vatican before the critical shift wiped out his empire. Huan Ken is very taken with old notions of chivalry and honor, but applies them selectively; at heart, he's still a greedy jerk, but he aspires to something better.

Li Ting, King of the Fire Pagoda

Li Ting is discussed on p. 204 of the rulebook. He's a heartless, amoral scumbag who openly admits that he intends to be the main beneficiary of any enterprise he's involved with. Li Ting is a master at manipulating human emotions, and spends most of his time with a look of stony placidity on his face.

Pui Ti, Queen of the Ice Pagoda

Perhaps the most sympathetic of the Four Monarchs, and yet the most stand-offish. She's the only one of the four to feel any guilt over the murder of their father, and she does what she can to keep the other three in check. More information on Pui Ti can be found on p. 204 of the rulebook.

ACT I: UPON A FEARFUL SUMMONS

The goal of this act is to set up the situation: something weird is going on with IKTV these days, and it's ticking off the Monarchs. There are no guaranteed fight scenes in this act, though the PCs may choose to involve themselves in the conflict that appears in scene 2.

Here's what's going down. A couple times in the last few weeks, a strange old Chinese man has been appearing on IKTV. He turns up in one show or another, usually taking the place of an existing character in the show. The show keeps going on, but the replaced character ignores the action to directly address the viewer; the other characters keep going as normal, as if the replaced character was still saying his or her lines as usual. The old man is funny to watch, since he insults the Monarchs. Few, if any, of IKTV's fans are allied with the Monarchs, and so this peculiar spectacle is a welcome diversion and a source of general amusement. Those who have noticed the old man's appearances assume it's some digital prankstersim on the part of the Towson twins. They're wrong.

SCENE 1: DON'T MAKE ME ANGRY

The only requirement for this scene is that the PCs be in the Netherworld, and that they be someplace where a television is. A good choice is the Genocide Lounge, described on p. 231 of the rulebook. In the afternoon, this happening nightspot is a mellow place to hang out, watch TV, and have some of the tasty gyros-and-feta omelettes that the Lounge's daytime short-order cook is known for. Alternately, the PCs may simply be passing through some Netherworld Rabble cluster of huts, where everyone is gathered around a shaped TV for easy entertainment. The Prof's junkyard also has a number of functioning televisions around, so if the PCs have to meet with her for some reason this option would work.

Whatever the situation, the important point is what's on the tube. It's an episode of a cheesy old American action-adventure series based on a comic book about a drifter who turns into a big muscle-bound green moron whenever he gets angry. Draw the PCs' attention to the screen. Here's what they see.

The big green guy is standing in a parking lot, looking directly at the camera. He looks different; his face, though still green, is that of an elderly Chinese man. Other actors get tossed around the screen, thrown by nothing at all. (Presumably, the big green guy would be kicking their butt but he's busy; they're still getting whupped on, but no one is doing the whupping at present.) The familiar voice of the green guy is replaced by the voice of an old man with a thick Chinese accent, but he still uses the diction and speech patterns of the super-hero character.

"Puny Monarchs! Huan Ken wear stupid pope hat! Huan Ken not fight way from paper bag! Ming stupid! Li stupid! Pui Ti stupid! King of nothing! Queen of nothing! Where father? Hah! No father! No father! Stupid Monarchs! Stupid! Smash! Smash!"

Anyone watching this besides the PCs bursts into laughter (and perhaps the PCs do, too). The viewers make comments that suggest this isn't the first time this has happened (i.e. "That old guy's slamming the Monarchs again!"). After the above diatribe, the big green guy's face returns and he goes back to kicking butt as usual.

If the PCs ask about this odd event, they'll learn that this weird old guy has been appearing on IKTV recently, maybe 3 or 4 times in the last couple of weeks. It's like he just takes over a character on whatever show is on and starts railing against the Monarchs. People are watching IKTV religiously, just to see this wacky guy appear. Viewers asked assume that those crazy Towson twins at IKTV are doing it to get the Monarchs' goat.

SCENE 2: THIS STORY IS TRUE

This scene occurs in the big Netherworld cavern that houses IKTV's headquarters, and specifically happens in front of the big twelve-story television screen that shows IKTV all day. The PCs may just be passing through on their way someplace else, or they might have arranged to meet someone here on some other business. IKTV is a major landmark, and there are always a bunch of **Ickies** (fanatical IKTV fans) around; they've set up tents, huts, and even shaped dwellings to stay near their beloved IKTV twelve-story screen, so it's easy to meet someone here clandestinely and use the crowd to keep the meeting secret.

At present, IKTV is showing an episode of *Unresolved Mysteries,* a popular true-crime show from America, hosted by a stone-faced and aging character actor who always wears a tan trenchcoat as if he himself is doing the legwork to solve the awful crimes featured this week. A big crowd of Ickies is gathered around the huge IKTV screen, lying on their backs like stoners at a Pink Floyd concert, enthralled by the mighty juggernaut of entertainment towering above them. As the PCs take in the scene, a group of a dozen foot soldiers loyal to Ming I, Queen of the Darkness Pagoda, come stomping in on their way someplace else.

On the screen, the stone-faced host of *Unresolved Mysteries* suddenly undergoes an identity shift: his face morphs into that of the elderly Chinese man seen in the first scene. This is, of course, the Monarchs' father. He speaks, in the clipped and stony diction of the show's host but with his own voice and accent:

"An old man, who thought he was safe in the world. Two sons and two daughters, of whom he was most proud. In the blink of an eye, the old man was dead. His murder—unresolved!"

The scene changes to show images of the Four Monarchs in turn.

"The suspects: Huan Ken, who foolishly named himself pope and worshipped chivalry while practicing cruelty; Li Ting, who divorced himself from morality and claimed there is no god; Pui Ti, whose sweet nature masked a terrible guilt; and Ming I, the Harlot of Darkness who calls her stupidity brilliance! Did one of these ignorant poltroons commit the crime?"

Anything else that the altered host has to say is lost; at the sound of the phrase "Harlot of Darkness," the foot soldiers raise an anguished cry and charge towards the big IKTV screen with destructive intent. The Ickies leap to their feet and gang up in front of the screen. A moment later, the two groups face off. A fight breaks out.

PC Apathy: If the PCs do nothing, the soldiers kick Ickie butt and kill several of the unfortunate rabble. Once their opposition is out of the way, the soldiers begin smashing the screen with their weapons and quickly destroy enough of the glass to short the whole thing out. The Towson sisters come running outside just long enough to see what's going on, then run inside the station and lock the door as a handful of Darkness soldiers race up and bang on it. They can't get in, and they quickly disperse to report to their Queen.

PC Valor: If the PCs intervene to save the unarmed Ickies or just to rumble, they'll be facing a dozen well-trained but unnamed Darkness soldiers who are enraged at the slur against their Queen. They're out for blood. Once half of the soldiers go down, the rest will retreat as best they can and inform Ming I of what happened. A ragged cry goes up from the Ickies and *Unresolved Mysteries* goes back to normal. The Towson sisters come out of the station and thank the PCs heartily; if the PCs haven't met Columbia and Laurel before, now's the time to introduce these GMCs. Feel free to foster a romantic interest if desired. The possible complications that can ensue should two PCs get involved with these identical twin sisters are left to the GM's imagination and knowledge of mistaken-identity movies. The Towsons can't explain what's going on with their broadcasts, but are not pleased with this manipulation of their baby.

Twelve Unnamed Darkness Soldiers
Sample Quote: "Eat humility, rabble!"
Distinguishing Features: Frenzied eyes, steely grins, Aztec-African clothing.
Attributes: Bod 6, Chi 1, Mnd 4, Ref 6
Skills: Intimidation 8, Martial Arts 8
Weapons: Sword (10)

CLOSING THIS ACT

The scenes of this act should both be over quickly, even if the PCs get into the fray in scene 2. However, there are a few things the GM should pay attention to, since they could affect future developments in this plotline.

Is Ming Ticked? If the PCs taught the soldiers a lesson in scene 2, Ming I is bound to hear of it. She won't be out for vengeance—she's more worried about this IKTV weirdness—but if she encounters the PCs again she'll keep their thrashing of her troops in mind and will not be favorably disposed to them. (As if she would be anyway…)

Are the Towsons Allies? If the PCs made friends with the Towson sisters, the Towsons may turn to them for help when IKTV gets ransacked in the next act.

Do the Players Care? If the players aren't responding well to these first two scenes, you might consider letting this sub-plot resolve itself off-screen and assume that all ends well. Lacking any initial curiosity or enthusiasm, the players may resent having their characters dragged into the story in the next act. If they aren't up for it, don't force it on them.

ACT II: THOUGH THIS BE MADNESS

In this act, the Monarchs get fed up and lash out at IKTV. Depending on the PCs' relationship with the Towsons this can go peacefully or can launch a big brawl. Whatever the case, it's discovered that someone has tampered with IKTV's equipment, allowing altered broadcasts to be fed in from some unknown location. Lusignan meets with the PCs briefly, giving nothing away except a strong hint of his involvement. Sometime later, the Monarchs figure out that the altered signals are coming by way of the Prof's junkyard, and Huan Ken arrests her for trial. The scene of the arrest almost certainly leads to a battle, but the Prof gets hauled off no matter what.

At the end of this act, the PCs should understand that the Towsons are innocent, that the Prof may be involved, and that Lusignan knows something about all this. Given the PCs' (presumed) relationship with the Prof, it'll be up to them to make the next move in act III; if they do nothing, the rest of the sub-plot plays out without their involvement in whatever manner you see fit.

SCENE 3: PLEASE STAND BY

This scene takes place at IKTV headquarters. The PCs can be wandering through here again, but it's much better if they have a reason to be here. If one or both of the Towsons have become friendly with the PCs, a summons from the sisters (relayed however you like) brings the PCs to the scene just in time. A low-level Netherworld friend of the PCs might also tell them that there's big trouble at IKTV, prompting the PCs to bust on over there like the good action heroes they are. Finally, if nothing else seems workable then have

Lusignan issue them a cryptic request for a meeting in the IKTV cavern; the meeting just happens to occur when the trouble goes down. (At this point in your campaign, handy coincidences like this one are probably falling like rain; if they aren't, you may be taking this all too seriously.) Lusignan meets with them at the end of the scene whether he summoned them or not. Note that Lusignan would have to send the PCs his request through a courier of some sort; like the Prof, the replacement Lusignan can't leave the Netherworld.

At IKTV, an unusual scene is unfolding: all four of the Monarchs are there, working together! Soldiers loyal to all four siblings are present, keeping the Ickies away from the station and mucking around inside the building. The Towsons are there, as well. Laurel is inside IKTV, 'helping' the soldiers ransack the building to figure out what's causing the strange manifestation. Columbia is outside in the cavern, held captive to ensure Laurel's participation in this process.

On the twelve-story IKTV television screen, the popular "reality-based drama" *Save Me 911* is playing. The mass of Ickies (several dozen, at least) press against the line of mixed-allegiance soldiers holding them back; half the Ickies are screaming about the invasion of IKTV, while the other half is screaming at the first half to shut up so they can watch the show.

Suddenly, it happens again. The overweight SciFi character actor that hosts the show morphs into the elderly Chinese man seen before. As usual, he retains the host character's diction while adding his voice and accent.

"Murder most… foul. Four… siblings. A family. A strong family. A… *strong*… family. Who killed the… father? This dramatic re-enactment shows… the truth."

The four monarchs look at the screen in horror as the scene of their father's death is played out as described on p. 201 of the rulebook. On screen, all four have obvious glee on their faces as they join forces to murder their father.

As the father dies on screen, Li Ting flies up in the air towards the top of the screen. He looks down and in a booming voice accuses Pui Ti of being responsible, blaming her guilt for making this revelation. He calls her all sorts of hideous names. Huan Ken zooms up to where Li Ting is and shouts back at his brother, calling him a fool for accusing their sister. Ming I joins them, siding with Li Ting, bellowing something insightful like "If she didn't do it, who did?" Finally Pui Ti flies up, too, and the four begin arguing in hushed voices so their followers do not hear them. It looks like all-out combat is about to start when the big IKTV screen goes blank.

A moment later, Laurel emerges from the building with a bunch of soldiers, holding a piece of electronics gear. She's found the source of the altered transmissions—a rebroadcast link that sends the signal to some other location, and then receives an altered signal back for broadcast. She has no idea who did this, or where the other half of the link is. She can, however, figure it out given time. The Monarchs calm down and return to ground; soon they depart, leaving behind a small group of guards to oversee the Towsons' attempts to trace the other half of the link. IKTV goes back on the air, without the ghost.

At least, that's how it goes if the PCs don't get involved.

If the PCs Intervene: Given the outline above, it should be relatively easy to adjudicate the action. The PCs might want to free the Towsons and attack the soldiers, or at least demand the twins' release. If so, use the soldier stats given for the Darkness troops in the previous act and let the PCs beat up whoever they feel like. At some point, however, the Monarchs will get involved and will bring the fight to a close one way or another; they're far more powerful than the PCs should be, and a brief demonstration of their power should bring an end to the battle and leave the PCs willing to negotiate. At any rate, whatever form of combat erupts should be allowed to continue until you have the Monarchs shut it down—and then, Laurel emerges from IKTV with the rebroadcast link and everyone chills out.

If the PCs Do Jack: Should the PCs stand silent and watch the scene unfold, it's not going to be very satisfying for the players (unless they're sitting around the table, slack-jawed and glassy-eyed in wonderment at your GMing prowess). So if that's all they're doing, start the following encounter with Lusignan *during* the scene rather than at the end (which is what the text otherwise assumes). That way, they get to interact with Lusignan a bit, and the PCs and Lusignan witness the argument between the Monarchs and the discovery of the mystery link.

ENTER LUSIGNAN

Lusignan the Fool is here (or rather, his automaton double is). He's in disguise, meaning that he's wearing a bunch of rags over his jester costume. When the scene is winding down, Lusignan gets a random GMC rabble member to bring the PCs over to where Lusignan waits in disguise, near an exit from the cavern.

Lusignan knows about the PCs from the Prof, and also knows that his link is about to be

discovered. He figures that the Monarchs will twig to the other half of the link being at the junkyard, but isn't certain; he wants to tip off the PCs that he knows something about what's going on so that they'll come to him if the shape hits the fan and the Prof needs help, but if that doesn't happen then he won't have incriminated himself too much.

The PCs' conversation with Lusignan is a typically-cryptic movie-style Deep Throat encounter: Lusignan will say something about the funny business with the Monarchs and IKTV and how maybe they'll figure it out. Which they? Figure what out? Lusignan shakes his head (ringing the bells in his cap) and says that if they figure it out, the PCs should probably look him up. Lusignan means, of course, that if the Monarchs figure out where the other half of the link is and get mad at the Prof, then the PCs should let Lusignan know. Get this across one way or another, but note that Lusignan won't mention the Prof, the junkyard, or his involvement in the situation; he'll just plant the idea that if things get weird, the PCs should look him up. That's all that's important.

SCENE 4: THINGS GET WEIRD

This scene requires that the PCs be at the junkyard with the Prof, and should occur at least a few days (if not a week or more) after the previous scene. If your group is meeting regularly with the Prof to discuss the secret war and to make plans, great. If not, you need a reason for the PCs to be there. You can either ask the players to decide on a reason themselves (a handy narrative tool indigenous to *Feng Shui*), or make one up. To help you out, here's one: the Prof has made a new gadget that she wants the PCs to try out. She's sent them a message asking them to drop by so she can show it to them.

At the Junkyard: The Prof's home is a large pile of discarded technology. There's all kinds of stuff, ranging from tiny circuit boards to wrecked tanks. It's perhaps the size of a football field (sometimes much bigger, sometimes much smaller!) with paths winding among the piles. Somewhere within, there's a secret entrance to the Prof's living quarters. She keeps her lab out in the junkyard, though, so that she always has parts close at hand.

The Gadget: If you're using the gadget as a macguffin to get the PCs to the scene, here's the scoop. The Prof has invented a device capable of detecting Netherworld gates. It only functions in the Netherworld at present—it's partially made of shaped items—but if it works, the Prof believes she can replicate it with real technology that will function in the real world. She'd like the PCs to take the gadget and try it out the next few times they're in the Netherworld. There's no rush. The gadget has nothing to do with this storyline, and will not be of particular aid to the PCs at present. (In fact, it may get them in big trouble if you want.) The gadget is described in more detail in the boxed text immediately below.

THE GATE SNIFFER

This device, created by the Prof, uses a modern-day cradle telephone as the case and in fact it looks like any telephone except that there are no cords; if taken apart, the case is full of weird glowing circuits and a chunk of pulsing organic material. When carried (even in a backpack), the phone will ring steadily whenever it is within fifty yards of a Netherworld gate, but only if the GM succeeds in an open roll of the phone carrier's Chi against a Difficulty of 10. (It functions even if in a backpack or briefcase; it's always functioning, even if the carrier doesn't particularly want it to.) The GM makes this roll in secret on behalf of the PC with the phone so that the players don't realize they're near a gate. The ringing of the phone is rather loud and it doesn't stop ringing until out of range of the gate. If the PCs are trying to be stealthy, the ringing phone will give their presence away. The Prof is assuming that the PCs won't be taking the phone into any trouble spots and so she hasn't worried about finding a more subtle means of announcing that a gate is nearby.

Should a smart-aleck PC pick up the handset when the phone is ringing, he hears a recording of the Prof's voice repeatedly saying "Hello. This phone is the property of the Prof. Please return it to the junkyard for a reward." Any PC who asks the Prof for the reward gets a poke in the ribs.

Since the phone's effectiveness is tied to the user's Chi score, the PCs may report back that the phone works great or that it doesn't work at all depending on who was carrying it. (The Prof doesn't realize this is the case.) If the phone found some gates, the Prof will be encouraged and may choose to develop versions in the future that will give direction, proximity, and a silent alarm. Whether or not this little experiment ultimately succeeds and how well it does so is up to the GM. Pay attention to which PC carries the phone during the rest of this sub-plot; it could give them away to nearby enemies by ringing, providing much GM amusement value and probably a gratuitous fight scene.

THUNDER KNIGHT TROUBLE

As the PCs are conferring with the Prof amongst the piles of debris in the junkyard, trouble comes to pay a call. A bunch of thunder knights (in the service of Huan Ken) arrive. They're led by Bishop Karras, one of the Thunder King's muckety-mucks but also a sorcerer of some power. With them is Laurel Towson from IKTV. The knights come waltzing into the junkyard through several of the paths at once, followed by Laurel and Karras. Laurel holds a device—she's looking for the rebroadcast link and the device has led her here.

Bishop Karras
Sample Quote: "His Holiness is not pleased."
Distinguishing Features: Medittaranean features, red robes, lots of gold rings.
Attributes: Bod 6, Chi 1 (Fu 8), Mnd 8, Ref 6
Skills: Leadership 10, Martial Arts 16
Fu Schticks: Prodigious Leap, Flying Windmill Kick, Clothed in Life, Natural Order
Weapons: Sword (10)

Thunder Knights, Warriors of Huan Ken
Sample Quote: "Stand aside, cretin!"
Distinguishing Features: European knightly armor, big swords, not too bright.
Attributes: Bod 6 (Tgh 8 with armor), Chi 1, Mnd 4, Ref 6 (Agl 5 with armor)
Skills: Intimidation 6, Martial Arts 10
Armor: Full suit of metal armor—Toughness +2, Agility -1
Weapons: Sword (10)

If the PCs Bust a Move: On seeing a crowd of armored thugs, the PCs may immediately attack without waiting for explanations. The knights aren't expecting a fight and will not be very effective fighters. However, the location makes fighting tricky: the paths through the junkyard are no more than three meters wide at most, and the knights are coming through three different paths. These paths empty into the Prof's lab area, an open if cluttered space about twenty meters in diameter. One PC can effectively cover (and fight in) each path, meaning that only three PCs can be in the front of the action; however, the PCs can choose to fall back and fight in the lab area. The lab is full of tables, counters, big power tools, and other goodies. Besides these options, a PC with jumping or flying powers could leap up on top of one of the piles of junk and from there have overhead access to all three paths at once for spells or missile weapons. There are two thunder knights per PC. After two sequences, Bishop Karras does an abundant leap onto a pile of debris and yells for everyone to stop; the knights retreat and Karras does his best to end this unwanted combat peacefully. Go on to the next section.

If the PCs Chill Out: Bishop Karras and Laurel Towson push through the menacing thunder knights and apologize for the intrusion. Karras explains that he is on a mission from His Majesty and Pope Huan Ken, King of Thunder. Laurel has traced the rebroadcast link here to the junkyard, and they intend to find it. The Prof tells them to go right ahead, insisting she knows nothing about this IKTV nonsense and couldn't care less. If the PCs object, the Prof calms them down and says she's sure they'll find nothing. She explains that there are all kinds of crazy signals coming out of the high-tech debris in her junkyard, and that's probably what Laurel is picking up. Laurel moves on to walk through the junkyard, accompanied by a thunder knight and perhaps a PC. If she's with a PC, Laurel says she's not at all happy about her current assign-

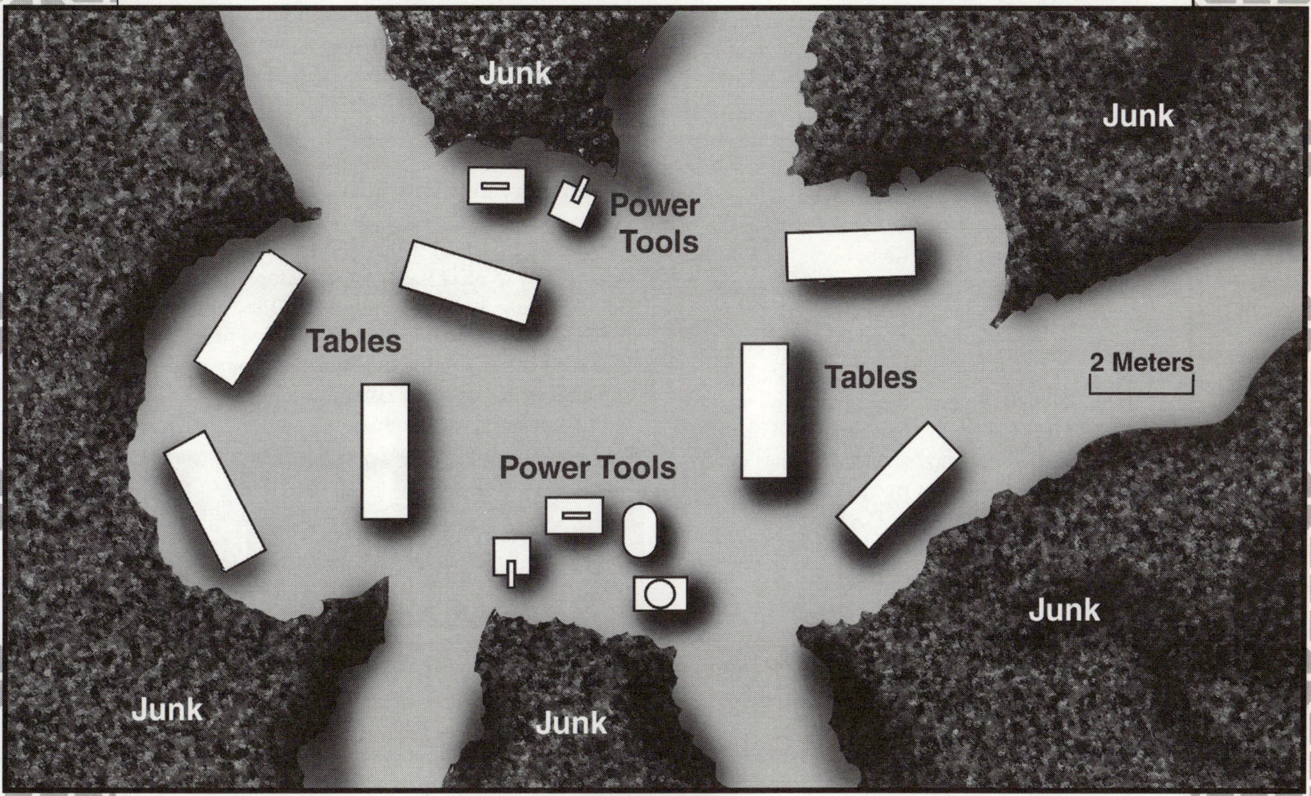

ment, but if she doesn't find the rebroadcast link she knows the Monarchs will lay waste to IKTV and perhaps to the sisters as well.

BUSTED!

Sure enough, Laurel hits paydirt. The rebroadcast link is in the junkyard, tucked inside a burned-out 1978 Ford LTD II. It's a big mass of equipment that takes up about half of the front seat; most of the bulk, however, comes from a weird crystal skull in the center that glows with an obviously-magical light. The skull has wires hooked up to it that run to the normal tech gear. Curiously, there's no sign of a video tape deck or other recording/playback unit. PCs with Fix-It skill can tell immediately that whatever alterations this equipment is making to IKTV's programming must be occurring live; it's not feeding altered videotapes of normal shows back into the system or anything. How this gear could be producing such dramatic changes to a live signal is tough to say, but it seems certain some form of magic is involved.

Bishop Karras tells the Prof that he has no choice but to place her under arrest and bring her back to the Thunder Pagoda for trial. (The charge? Sedition! Slander! Libel! One of those things!) The Prof is willing to go, but the PCs may not be willing to let her. If a fight breaks out here, refer to the information under "If the PCs Bust a Move" earlier in the text to adjudicate it. However, Karras will enter the fight immediately. He will not try to kill any PC; he just wants to beat them into surrendering so he can take off with the Prof. The thunder knights will not be so kind, especially if they've already been kicked around some; on the other hand, the PCs will probably wipe up the floor with them. Laurel stays out of the fray, and is obviously not pleased with the way things are going; the Prof has helped the Towsons out before with repairs at IKTV, and the sisters consider her an ally.

Peacemaker: The Prof does *not* want a fight to break out. She'll do her best to calm the PCs down and state that she is willing to go with Karras. She says she knows nothing whatsoever about the rebroadcasting equipment or how it came to be in the junkyard, but that she knows Huan Ken to be an honorable man (well no, he's not, but the Prof knows that Huan Ken likes to be thought of that way) and that she has every expectation of being set free by the generous and noble Monarch. If the PCs object, she makes a persuasive argument: if the PCs hack off the Thunder King, they can just scuttle back to their world and not have to worry about it too much; but the Prof has to *live* here, and she cannot do so if the Thunder King wants her head on a stick because the PCs waxed a bunch of knights and killed a bishop.

Even if a fight breaks out, the Prof should be able to bring things to a halt through whatever dramatic means you see fit to employ. If the PCs are determined to fight, the Prof whips out some gadget from the lab that showers huge globs of sticky goo all over the combat area. It works like the Glutinous Goo effect of the Foul Spew creature ability (p. 127 in the rulebook), but use the Prof's Fix-It score of 20 as the AV. This brings the fight to a halt, and the Prof reasons with the PCs and the thunder knights alike. A sequence after the PCs agree to let her go with Karras, the goo evaporates into nothing. (How's that for *goous ex machina*?)

Come the end of the scene, Karras and the remaining knights march off to the Thunder Pagoda with the Prof in tow. The PCs are not welcome to come along.

CLOSING THIS ACT

This act ends with the Prof getting hauled off to the Thunder Pagoda, there to face a trial for dishonoring the Monarchs with altered IKTV signals. The Towsons are free of danger now, however, and IKTV is broadcasting as normal. Lusignan has advised the PCs to contact him if things get weird, and that's just what has happened; the crystal skull might also serve as a hint to the PCs that Lusignan (who favors skull and clown-face decor) may be involved, but it's a weak hint at best. Points you should consider before you wrap up include:

- **Did the PCs get the gist** of their meeting with Lusignan? If it isn't clear to them that they need to see him soon (perhaps immediately), you'll need to have Lusignan summon them to his tower instead.
- **Is Huan Ticked?** Huan Ken will not be happy to hear about any of his followers getting deep-sixed by the PCs. If they got trigger-happy and started spilling blood, the Thunder King will demand an apology the next time he encounters the PCs.
- **Are the Towsons Still Allies?** The PCs may not respond well to Laurel's aiding the Monarchs, especially if the PCs haven't had an opportunity to meet the Towsons before. If that's the case, keep this in mind for the future—it'll be tough for the Towsons to make nice with the PCs in the future if the group is still smoldering over the sisters' compliance with the Monarchs' demands.

ACT III: THE CONSCIENCE OF THE KING

This final act is in the PCs' hands. They need to meet with Lusignan to see what he has to say, and then they need to be present at the Prof's trial. The trial can be staged whenever it's convenient for your campaign. It might be the same day that the Prof is arrested, or it can the following day, the next week, or whatever you like.

© 1996 Heather Hudson

SCENE 5: THE COURT JESTER

The PCs should know that they need to go see Lusignan, owing to their brief meeting with him in act II. If the meeting didn't happen, Lusignan summons them through a message of some sort. The meeting occurs as soon as the PCs want it to.

Lusignan's Tower is a well-known Netherworld landmark. Standing four stories tall, this sturdy edifice is covered in giant carven skulls and clown faces. Lusignan lives within, and rarely ventures outside. The cavern in which the tower stands is otherwise empty, and few go there.

Arriving at the tower, the PCs have only to knock at the great door that stands in the tower's base. The door swings open, and a voice from higher up in the tower bids them enter. Ascending the spiral staircase through rooms littered with odds and ends, the PCs enter Lusignan's chambers. He awaits them in a large room two stories up, decorated in the skull-and-clown motif seen outside. Lusignan sits in a big wooden chair with claw feet, watching IKTV on a black-and-white television.

The jester springs out of his chair and greets the PCs. His conversation with them is up to you to adjudicate, but these are the major points he wants to get across:

- The rebroadcast link is his doing. The Prof and the Towson twins knew nothing about it. He snuck into IKTV and set up half the gear there.
- He put the other half in the junkyard because he needed access to some of the Prof's gear there. He also thought that all the electronic interference generated by the Prof's equipment would disguise the location of the link.
- He wanted to teach the Monarchs a lesson in humility.
- The alterations to IKTV's programming weren't created by Lusignan. They were created by the Monarchs' own collective guilt over murdering their father centuries ago, when he refused to crown them as the kings and queens of the world. The crystal skull in the link drew on the guilt-influenced chi energy of the Monarchs and altered the broadcasts accordingly—the Monarchs were torturing themselves. Lusignan only made it possible.
- He will not go to the trial. He says Huan Ken would not tolerate his presence. (Lusignan is lying. He suspects that Huan Ken could tell that Lusignan isn't the real thing, and he's not willing to let that happen.)

- He has something for the PCs to take to the trial. It's a human skull, ancient and worn with age. This is the skull of the Monarchs' father, which Lusignan stole from Huan Ken's court years ago and replaced with a fake. The crystal skull used in the rebroadcast link is a magical duplicate of this one.
- He tells the PCs that they'll need to summon the spirit of the Monarchs' father at the trial, using the skull as a focus.
- He asks the PCs to offer the Prof his apologies for the confusion.

Anything else Lusignan has to say is up to you. He will not go to the trial under any circumstances, though he'll be happy to let the PCs reveal his involvement at the trial if they want to. He will not reveal his relationship with the Prof, or admit that he's not the real Lusignan.

Lusignan should always sound a bit cracked. He's not entirely sane, and he tends to use a mocking, servile tone of speech. Have him say crazy things and non sequiturs as much as you like; the PCs should get the clue that Lusignan isn't playing with a full deck but doesn't mean any real harm. Still, he should also come off as pretty crafty.

Whenever he's said all he wants to say, Lusignan declares the meeting over in an imperious fashion. He tells the PCs they can show themselves out.

GETTING READY

The PCs will need to be able to summon the ghost of the Monarchs' father from the skull. Doing this requires the use of the Invocation special effect of the Summoning magic schtick. If no PC has Summoning, they need to find someone who does. A GMC ally could do this. If they don't know anyone, allow them to check with their contacts, ask around the Netherworld, or whatever. If you need a GMC sorcerer to do the job, one is provided in the next section who will cooperate in exchange for a reasonable payment for her services. Lusignan can suggest her if the PCs ask about it during their meeting.

Jana Anderson, Sorcerer for Hire

This resident of the Netherworld is a competent but not exceptional sorcerer in her late forties. She has lived here for years, after her timestream (the same as the Monarchs') was wiped out by a critical shift. Jana knows the Monarchs well, having grown up in the world they ruled; they don't know her, however. She doesn't like the Monarchs very much and will gladly agree to the PCs' request.

The PCs might want to summon the spirit of the Monarchs' father before the trial, just to make sure it works and to secure his cooperation. This isn't necessary, but it doesn't hurt. The summoning attempt automatically succeeds, though the sorcerer should still make the roll.

The ghost appears. (Like every human being on the planet, he looks thinner in real life than he did on TV.) He's not happy about being disturbed, but once the PCs explain the score, he'll be happy to cooperate. He tells the PCs to summon him again at the trial, and he'll deal with his foolish children.

Jana Anderson
Sample Quote: "I've got that powder here somewhere… "
Distinguishing Features: Weary look, simple clothes, grin.
Attributes: Body 6, Chi 2 (Magic 4), Mind 7, Reflexes 6
Skills: Info/Netherworld 10, Sorcery 11
Magic Schticks: Divination, Heal, Summoning

SCENE 6: THE TRIAL

The trial of the Prof is held in the Thunder Pagoda. Spectators are allowed. In a moment of goofy chivalry, Huan Ken told the Towsons that they can broadcast the trial live over IKTV; he wants the entire Netherworld to know that the Towsons are innocent, and that the real culprit is someone else.

Arriving at the pagoda, the PCs can take their seats with a crowd of perhaps twenty onlookers. The trial is being held in Huan Ken's royal court. Numerous thunder knights and bishops are present, as are the other three Monarchs and their retainers. Columbia and Laurel Towson are here with a camera, lights, and other gear for the live broadcast. The sisters argue briefly about who gets to be in front of the camera; Columbia wins, and gives a brief report on IKTV before the trial begins.

If the PCs mixed it up with the thunder knights or the darkness soldiers in earlier scenes, both Huan Ken and Ming I give the PCs unpleasant glares.

ENTER THE PROF

Huan Ken opens the trial with an official statement. He states the facts of the case plainly—that someone was altering IKTV's broadcasts and filling them with lies and insults against him and his siblings—and then explains that someone had set up a rebroadcasting link at IKTV and at the Prof's junkyard. Huan Ken addresses the room, but he spends most of the time looking straight at the IKTV camera, beaming like a politician on CNN.

Without further ado, the Prof is brought in by two thunder knights and seated in a chair in the middle of the hall. She looks a bit nervous but does not appear to have been mistreated during her incarceration. Ming I hisses at her. Pui Ti looks sad. Li Ting's face is stolid and unemotional.

A thunder bishop strides forward and asks a few questions. Was the Prof inside IKTV shortly before the strange broadcasts began? "Yes, I was making some repairs at the request of the Towsons." Does the Prof have the knowledge, skills, and equipment to have assembled and implemented the rebroadcast link? "Yes, I do." Is the Prof the sole resident of the junkyard? "Yes, I am." Is she responsible for the rebroadcast link? "No, I'm not." The bishop has no further questions.

So much for the trial. Huan Ken asks the assembled crowd if anyone has anything to say before he passes judgement. It's time for the PCs to make their move.

ENTER THE GHOST

The PCs can preface their summoning of the spirit however they like. They might want to get up and say something about a surprise witness, yadda yadda yadda. Or they might just cast the spell and get the show on the road.

Either way, the spirit of the father erupts from the skull. The Monarchs, even Li Ting, drop their jaws in shock and the blood drains out of their faces. Sure, they know their father's spirit was bumping around somewhere—but they hadn't expected to see him in the flesh, so to speak.

How this scene plays out is up to you to describe, since it would be a bit tacky to read the climax of the storyline straight from this book. Essentially, the father is ticked off at his children. He berates them for being fools, and for losing control of the world in such a stupid fashion. He tells them it serves them right to be exiled in the Netherworld with the rest of the rabble—they took the gift of his knowledge and squandered it. He says they dishonored themselves by killing their own father out of petty jealousy. He's been in the Underworld ever since, atoning for his own mistakes, but not any more: he's free of that wretched place, and he has plans for the world of the living. They'll be hearing from him again in the future.

The Monarchs' faces are ashen. It's been centuries since their old man gave them what for.

Finally, the spirit addresses the PCs and the crowd. He tells how he refused to crown his children as the kings and queens of the world, and how they worked together—for once—and murdered him in cold blood. By the way, they're a bunch of fools and he expresses his sincere sorrow for those who have to share the Netherworld with this pack of crawling vermin.

Unless the PCs have something to ask him, the spirit rebukes his children one final time and fades away, looking stern.

The Prof stands up. "May I leave now?" Huan Ken nods, his face a mask of humiliation. The other Monarchs don't say a word, but they all look intensely uncomfortable. The Prof heads over to the PCs and suggests that they leave quickly. As they do, Columbia Towson is jabbering into the camera about the surprise witness and the terrible revelation "made live right here on IKTV, your number one source for news in the Inner Kingdom!"

WRAPPING UP

Presumably, the PCs have cleared the Prof and made fools of the Monarchs. The siblings are unusually quiet for some weeks, making no public appearances and staying within their pagodas, brooding and ticked off. They'll like the PCs even less than before, but they won't be out for vengeance—they got what they deserved and they know it.

The PCs have the skull of the Monarchs' father, unless they left it at the trial. Assuming they have it, the Prof asks for it once they're well away from the Thunder Pagoda. She says she'll take it back to Lusignan. Given that the PCs have probably not told her where they got it from, this may come as a surprise; clever players should pick up on this and ask how the Prof knew where it came from. "A woman knows these things," she says, and that's her final answer.

FURTHER ADVENTURES

- Of the Four Monarchs, only the guilt-stricken Pui Ti is likely to harbor no grudges against the PCs. If they get involved with her at some point in the future, she thanks them for what they did at the trial.
- Ming I is likely to harbor a major grudge against the PCs down the road, especially if they also tangled with her soldiers. She won't seek revenge for its own sake, but will jump at any opportunity to hose the PCs.
- Ditto for Li Ting, only more so. He might actually pursue vengeance against the PCs, if you think you need a major villain to cause trouble for your group.
- Huan Ken will not be eager to see the PCs again, but he won't stay mad at them. His on-again, off-again sense of chivalry will in this case work in the PCs' favor, as he believes they only did what they had to do.
- Lusignan and the PCs will now have gotten introduced if they hadn't before. Try and keep him out of the campaign for a while if possible; he works best if taken in small doses.
- If the Towsons end this storyline on good terms with the PCs, they may contact the PCs in the future if they need help or just a date. They may have business in the real world to take care of, and could draw the PCs into adventures there.

EXT. SHAOLIN MONASTERY COURTYARD (1850 A.D.)—MORNING

We're somewhere in rural China. It's a clear day, and the courtyard is a beautiful assembly of statues, grass, and trees. Three monks in white robes walk closely together in measured paces. They are CHUN CHANG, a young warrior-monk: he's tall, lean, shaven, glassy-eyed; ELDER BROTHER TZU-YEH, a deputy abbot of respected age with a drooping black mustache, intemperate manner, and rotund belly; and THE REVERED MASTER SSU-MA-NIU, of unknowable age, short, his arms hidden in voluminous sleeves, his eyes glittering, his smile serene.

CHUN CHANG

I cannot stop thinking of her. I meditate, and her heavenly eyes appear before me. Her full lips—

ELDER BROTHER TZU-YEH

Yes, yes, we take your meaning.

THE REVERED MASTER SSU-MA NIU

May one ask how so diligent a monk deserted his practice and became smitten, like a drunken poet?

CHUN CHANG

I rode into the mountains to bring medicines to a party ambushed by bandits. The bandits themselves ambushed me. I dispatched six, but the others overcame me. Then from the trees above came a musical shout, and she swept down—

TZU-YEH

A "musical shout"!

SSU-MA NIU

Peace, brother, passion colors his memory. So this warrior woman rescued you, brother?

CHUN CHANG

And then she stared into my eyes, and I into hers. In that moment I glimpsed the higher meditative states, or perhaps even nirvana—

TZU-YEH

You fell into a senseless infatuation, the opposite of clear perception. Now that this woman, this Kam Li, has passed into the Netherworld, note how your attachment provokes suffering. Reflect on—

SSU-MA NIU

May the deputy abbot delay his worthy lesson a moment longer? What took Kam Li to the Netherworld?

CHUN CHANG

I learned this from one of the surviving bandits. She pursued their employer, a detestable Cambodian sorcerer named Phanom Rung. He had stolen a stone of some kind that would harness powerful magic, depending on how long it lay underground. So he buried it in the foothills, then journeyed forward to the Hong Kong of the next century—

TZU-YEH

—a lawless city, maddened by greed and luxury—

CHUN CHANG

—where he would uncover the stone, now grown rich in power. Kam Li followed him to prevent this. But she has been gone a week now, and her absence worries me deeply. To think of that fair woman, fallen prey to a ruthless and evil magician, her beautiful head drooping limply on her shapely neck—

SSU-MA NIU

(cutting him short)

A tragedy, yes. Tell me, brother, do you know the nature of this stone?

CHUN CHANG

I know only its name—the Stone of Roaring Winds.

SSU-MA NIU

(thunderstruck)

No! It cannot be! The Windstone, buried in Hong Kong!

TZU-YEH

One gathers that you know of—?

SSU-MA NIU

Quickly, the both of you! We leave at once for the Netherworld gate!

ALLEN VARNEY

SHAOLIN HEARTBREAK

ILLUSTRATED BY JON WEIMAN

Premise: A lovestruck Shaolin monk from 1850 journeys to the contemporary juncture to rescue the warrior woman he loves from an evil sorcerer. The PCs choose sides and fight.
The Twist: The warrior woman is a dead ringer for a celebrity pop singer involved with the PCs.
The Climax: Everyone fights it out on Kai Tak Airport's Runway One during a typhoon. Yes, really.

BACKSTORY

A Betak sorcerer-king named Balabac crafted and buried a powerful magical talisman on the Philippine island of Palawan between 1550 and 1580. Balabac meant the Stone of Roaring Winds to drive away Muslim missionaries by luring typhoons to their port town of Labog. Before the Stone could achieve significant power, Spain conquered the island and killed the sorcerer-king. Balabac's son, fearing the Stone's power, dug it up and fled with it to Canton (Kuangchou).

The Stone went through many hands, the way these mind-bendingly powerful artifacts usually do, and wound up in Cambodia in 1850. Learning of the Stone almost by accident, the ancient sorcerer **Phanom Rung** killed its previous owner and stole it. "With this stone," Rung thought, "I shall wipe from the Earth, once and for all, those nuisance monks of Shaolin!"

THE CAST AND THE SET-UP

For six centuries Rung had practiced his dark alchemy unhindered, first for the Khmer god-king Jayavarman and later for his own evil ends. But through their control of feng shui sites and suppression of the chi flow, the Guiding Hand made his alchemy more difficult. Now Rung plans to use the Stone's magic to destroy their sites, and incidentally most of Hong Kong, in a titanic typhoon.

The Stone doesn't create typhoons; it just attracts them, as a lodestone attracts iron, once the owner buries it. Unfortunately for Rung, the Stone requires many decades to build up the magic needed to guide a hurricane's path. Fortunately for Rung, he knows about the Netherworld and the contemporary juncture.

Rung's scheme: In 1850, Rung travelled to Hong Kong and buried the Stone in a remote part of the mainland wilderness. He intended to journey forward 146 years and retrieve the artifact after it had built up a huge charge, then carry it back to 1850 and rebury it. (The Stone keeps its charge as long as it's buried in the same place.) Then the Hand's feng shui sites would be devastated by repeated typhoons, and Rung could move in and control them himself.

Rung's mistake: In the small port of Hong Kong, Rung stopped to eat at a rice stall. He behaved with his usual arrogance, took offense when the owner accidentally spilled sake on his robes, and began beating her. Another customer at the stall—the warrior woman and innerwalker **Kam Li**—protected the owner, and she and Rung fought. Rung bested Li, but had to flee a gathering mob before he could kill her.

Having used so many powders, Rung needed funds to purchase more ingredients. He mentally dominated a rabble of rowdy thugs and set about robbing travellers outside the village. Meanwhile, Kam Li tracked him. Bandits and warrior clashed in the forest, while Rung was away searching for a Netherworld gate. By chance a young monk of the Guiding Hand, **Chun Chang**, got caught between the combatants. After years isolated from women, the impressionable young monk saw the beautiful Kam Li in action and instantly fell in love.

Forward to 1996: After the fight, Li left Chang without a backward glance and raced through the Netherworld gate after the sorcerer. She caught up with Rung in modern-day Hong Kong, where the changed terrain (flattened hills, land reclaimed from the sea) confused Rung's memory of where he'd buried the Stone. He had a map to its site, but Kam Li stole it. However, in battle she fell victim to his Powder of Wandering Impulse (a cool name for his Influence magic schtick).

Now confused and amnesic, Kam Li roams the congested back alleys of HK. Chun Chang and two elder monks of the Hand, **Tzu-Yeh** and **Ssu-ma Niu**, have travelled to the present to find her. Phanom Rung, severely wounded in battle, has spent a week healing and is now ready to find Kam Li, get his map back, and regain the Stone of Roaring Winds.

Where the heroes come in: By an amazing coincidence, Kam Li is the spitting image of popular HK pop singer and movie star **Maureen Wei**. The player characters (PCs) may be Maureen's bodyguards, managers, roadies, fans, or lovers. When the vengeful Phanom Rung and the heartstruck Chun Chang both mistake Maureen for Kam Li, the PCs get caught in the middle. The scene is set for mistaken identities, romantic triangles, and, of course, action, action, action.

Meanwhile, off shore, **Typhoon Jason** grows in strength...

GMC NOTES

Here are descriptions of the main GM characters in the story:

Maureen Wei

Maureen grew up poor in the crowded Mongkok neighborhood of Kowloon. Her lovely voice and good looks got her work as a lounge singer at the sprawling nightclubs China City and Club Volvo, and from there she made it big with a recording contract with Silver Moon Records. After her 1992 single "Marked for Love" made an Abundant Leap up the pop charts, Maureen got some martial arts training and went into movies. In her latest film, "Splendid City II: The Warriors Return," Maureen reprises her starring role as Kang-Hsi, a tragic warrior who fights to oust the British from 1850s China.

Maureen can become a romantic interest for one or more male PCs. Play her as cheeky and perhaps a bit vain, but professional, congenial, intelligent, and respectful of the PCs' abilities. Maureen quickly accepts the strangeness of this adventure's events and sensibly tries to win over a PC as her protector against Phanom Rung. She's as surprised as anyone when she falls in love with her protector.

Note: The big surprise at the end of this adventure is that Maureen Wei is actually the reincarnation of Kam Li. Keep this secret until the final fight.

Maureen Wei
Sample Dialogue: "Wait, what's—whoa! Would someone please tell me—hey! Stop swinging that thing at—yow!"
Distinguishing Features: Shining black hair, arching eyebrows, straight nose, cleft chin, mole on left jaw
Attributes: Body 4, Chi 0 (Fortune 6), Mind 4 (Charisma 8), Reflexes 4
Skills: Driving 6, Info/Showbiz 14, Martial Arts 6, Seduction 14

Kam Li

The year 1850, Kam Li's 24th birthday, found the Cantonese warrior woman frustrated at heart. For years she had tracked the seven officials who, many years before, had killed Kam Li's father. The elder Kam had been the finest swordmaker in the province. For daughter Li's tenth birthday he had given her a marvelous sword named Serpent Strike, which could slice through solid steel. But that same day he ran afoul of corrupt civil servants who tried to "confiscate" his valuable weapons. Struggling against them, the old man died by his own blades.

The heartsick child fled town and devoted her life to the study of martial arts, shutting away thoughts of men and of love. She returned home years later to exact her vengeance. But after killing six of the officials, she found the seventh already dead—for this magistrate happened to own the Stone of Roaring Winds, and Phanom Rung had murdered him for it.

Now Kam Li seeks Phanom, who stole her rightful vengeance and, she begins to realize, is a danger to all China. The warrior woman has tried not think of what she will do once Phanom Rung is destroyed and her quest completed. She yearns to help her people, but wonders if she herself is beyond help. After her years of violence, can she ever resume a peaceful life? Is there a man anywhere that she can believe worthy of her love?

Kam Li
Sample Dialogue: "Free that old woman! Abundant Leap! Ki-aaaa!"
Distinguishing Features: Shining black hair, arching eyebrows, straight nose, cleft chin, mole on left jaw
Attributes: Body 5, Chi 7, Mind 5, Reflexes 7
Skills: Info/Secret War 8, Info/Sorcery 10, Intimidation 8, Intrusion 9, Martial Arts 14, Medicine 9
Fu Powers: Prodigious Leap, Abundant Leap, Flying Sword, Water Sword
Weapons: punch (6), kick (7), Serpent Strike (signature sword, base damage 12), six throwing stars, two sais (daggers, base damage 8)

Phanom Rung

The year 1850, Phanom Rung's 700th birthday, found the Khmer sorcerer still healthy and vigorous. Sounds great, until you realize that he spent 650 of those years in unceasing alchemical life-extension research.

Though he's spent most of his centuries alone in the upland jungles of Laos, Rung has gotten annoyed at the falling magic levels and has decided to get involved in the secret war. In theory he just wants to wipe out the Guiding Hand, restore the magic level, and then go home. But his ruthlessness and incredible arrogance bring him into conflict with nearly everyone in his way.

Rung is tall and broadly built, looks about 45, and wears an ornate blue tunic split down the front to expose his muscled chest. He has filmy white cataracts on his eyes, but sees perfectly using magic. Along a wide dandelion-yellow sash at his waist hang many small moleskin pouches, each with a different powder or granular material (dust, seeds, ground metal). Most of Rung's spells rely on these powders; without them, he falls back on his powers to dominate and hypnotize unwilling minions. When Rung exerts his Influence magic, his white eyes turn first pink, then (as he uses more power) deeper and deeper red.

A note on the pouches: If anyone besides Rung tries to look or reach inside one of his pouches, the pouch delivers a Blast of damage 12-Toughness (automatic success).

Chun Chang

Good-hearted Chun Chang has spent his 22 years within the Shaolin Temple, preparing to serve the Guiding Hand. He excels in the rigorous discipline of the martial arts and knows something of the secret war, but otherwise has learned almost nothing of the world. In particular, he knows little of women, and so when he met Kam Li in the forest, he was unprepared for sudden infatuation. (But then again, is anyone ever prepared?)

Chang wishes to obey his masters, be a good monk, and marry Kam Li; he avoids thinking about the mutual exclusivity of these goals. Open attacks on the Hand would arouse his anger, but during this adventure Chang may come to doubt both his faction's methods and his chosen vocation.

Tzu-Yeh

Tzu-Yeh has served as deputy abbot of Shaolin Temple for decades. Though authoritarian, complacent, intolerant, and gruff, he is not cruel or malign. Like most of the Hand, he simply never considers that anything outside China can be important. He spends most of this adventure either fighting or complaining about his digestion.

Ssu-ma Niu

You've seen the standard Aged Asian Martial Arts Master in a dozen movies and TV shows. This is

Phanom Rung
Sample Dialogue: "Impudence! Puny underling, heed the lesson of my Dust of Enslavement!"
Distinguishing Features: Coppery skin, bulging forehead, filmy white eyes
Attributes: Body 6 (Tgh 10), Chi 6 (Magic 10), Mind 6 (Will 10), Reflexes 6
Skills: Info/The Occult 13, Intimidation 11, Medicine 12, Sorcery 18
Magic Schticks: Blast (base damage 12; special effects Acid, Disease, Transmutation), Divination, Heal, Influence, Movement, Summoning
Cool Effect Names: Constricting Heart Powder (Blast), Far-Seeing Rice Grains (Divination), Kernels of Healthful Vigor (Heal), Powder of Wandering Impulse (Influence), Powdered Wings (Movement), Demon Seeds (Summoning)

Chun Chang
Sample Dialogue: "So—so, um, are you, ah, married?"
Distinguishing Features: Tall, bald, nervous manner
Attributes: Body 7, Chi 9, Mind 3, Reflexes 8
Skills: Info/Secret War 8, Martial Arts 14
Fu Powers: Prodigious Leap, Abundant Leap, Flying Windmill Kick, Clothed in Life, Armored in Life, Hands Without Shadow, Dim Mak
Weapons: punch (8), kick (9), staff (base damage 10)

Tzu-Yeh
Sample Dialogue: "This barbarous future time is full of miscreants. I wish I might enlighten them with a hammer."
Distinguishing Features: Bald, stout, black mustache
Attributes: Body 5, Chi 10, Mind 5, Reflexes 7
Skills: Info/Secret War 10, Martial Arts 15
Fu Powers: Prodigious Leap, Abundant Leap, Flying Windmill Kick, Clothed in Life, Armored in Life, Hands Without Shadow, Dim Mak
Weapons: punch (6), kick (7), staff (base damage 8)

Ssu-ma Niu
Sample Dialogue: "May one ask how the respected gunman intends to find his target in the midst of a typhoon?"
Distinguishing Features: Bald, tuft of white beard on his chin
Attributes: Body 6, Chi 11, Mind 6, Reflexes 6
Skills: Info/Secret War 12, Leadership 10, Martial Arts 16, Medicine 10
Fu Powers: Prodigious Leap, Abundant Leap, Flying Windmill Kick, Clothed in Life, Armored in Life, Hands Without Shadow, Dim Mak
Weapons: punch (7), kick (8), staff (base damage 9)

Mooks
Phanom Rung magically dominated these hoods, making them even stupider and more brutal than usual. The controlled mooks have glazed white eyes, like the sorcerer himself.

Mooks
Sample Dialogue: "Hnnnh."
Attributes: Body 6, Chi 0, Mind 4, Reflexes 5
Skills: Guns 7, Martial Arts 7
Weapons: punch (7), kick (8), revolver (9/2/6)

THE BIT PLAYERS

Maureen's agent and manager is a servile nebbish named **Larry Kwan**. He's short, balding, wears dark suits with loud ties and pearl cufflinks, and smokes foul cigars. In this adventure Larry runs dull but necessary errands, passes along clues the PCs didn't find, and generally expedites the journey between fight scenes. Larry can also be a minor nuisance in a fight or a handy hostage for a bad guy.

Later in the adventure, the PCs visit Mongkok, where Maureen knows an old geomancer named **Chu Po**. See Scene 3 for his description.

GETTING STARTED

Manager Larry Kwan provides a convenient way to gather all the PCs in Victoria Park as the adventure begins. He hires some of them as bodyguards, and knows others from his school days. As for the rest, Larry gives them invitations to the Victoria Park event that is kicking off Maureen's new promotional tour (and the adventure). Larry doesn't even have to know the PCs; he might have just handed out the invitations on a street corner to passersby.

If this pretext doesn't work, PCs may simply be visiting the park on their own. They might be keeping an appointment, socializing, or going down to practice their martial arts among hordes of Tai Chi students.

At least one PC should have a reason to protect Maureen. Does a male PC have a crush on her?

SCENE 1: VICTORIA PARK

It's a threatening morning in September. On the way to Victoria Park in eastern Hong Kong, the PCs can look down at Causeway Bay and see the typhoon shelter. Behind the concrete barricade, sampans float crowded together, and more arrive as the PCs watch. The characters know that Typhoon Jason is two days away across the South China Sea. Although it's not raining here—yet—the sea is choppy and winds are gusty. No one can say if the storm will hit HK.

Just off Causeway Bay across busy Victoria Park Avenue lies the avenue's 18-acre namesake, one of the largest patches of open ground in HK. All around stand department stores, camera shops, florists, boutiques, and, in the back streets behind the Excelsior Hotel, garment factory outlets with sweatshops above. Victoria Park isn't much to look at, but it has tennis courts, small pitches for cricket and football (i.e., soccer), and a couple of swimming pools. Taking their caged songbirds for an airing, elderly but dignified men hang the cages from manicured trees, then sit on the wooden benches below.

OPENING SCENE

In the park's largest open space, Golden Phoenix Studios has set up an open-sided canvas tent with an elevated wooden dais and rank upon rank of steel folding chairs. Hundreds of movie fans fill the tent, standing room only. To one side of the dais stands Larry Kwan, smiling smugly and puffing on a cigar. "This is going great," he tells a PC. "We'll be all over tonight's news."

Amid a dizzying strobe of flashbulb bursts, Maureen Wei stands at a lectern emblazoned with the studio logo, surrounded by microphones, photographers, and whirring video cameras. Dressed as Kang-Hsi, her character in *Splendid City II,* Maureen wears a uniform of white cotton, with gold trim and a sun hat. Her costume looks exactly—you knew this was coming—exactly like the warrior woman Kam Li's cotton outfit.

The sorcerer Phanom Rung saw Maureen's costumed image on a poster announcing this promotional event and, weak on the concept of film stars, mistook her for Kam Li. He promptly enslaved a bunch of Kowloon thugs and told them to grab the warrior woman. Phanom Rung is hanging back outside the park, watching. He expects that Kam Li will handily mop up the goons, but hopes that one or two will land a lucky blow and soften her up. The tent and the crowds baffle the sorcerer, but he doesn't care about them. He just wants the map Kam Li carries, the map that tells the location of the Stone of Roaring Winds.

By a startling coincidence, the three monks of the Guiding Hand saw the same poster, made the same mistake, and are coming to Victoria Park for the same reason.

THE TENT

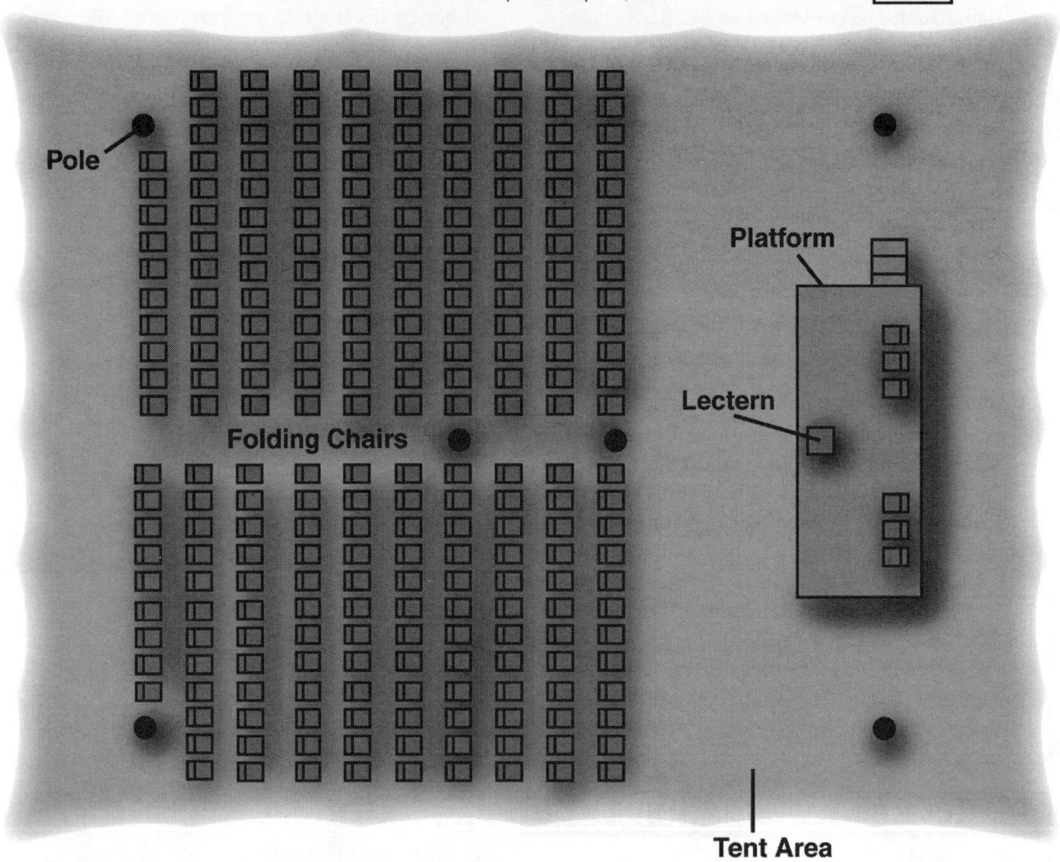

PARK FIGHT

As Maureen talks about "Fated for Love," the new song she sings in her movie, the PCs notice the thugs moving in from all sides. There are three thugs for each PC, plus three more; they're standard-issue dumb hoods in cheap sportcoats and sunglasses, without identifying marks. Ordinarily they might try to look innocent (by thug standards), maybe by munching on skewers of teriyaki chicken or pretending to be a cricket team. But while dominated by Phanom Rung, these mooks haven't got even this much subtlety.

If the PCs weren't around, the hoods would pull their revolvers, get the audience to squat where they stand, then grab Maureen and run with her to their waiting cars.

Remind the players that (a) there are innocent bystanders everywhere, and (b) there are also cameras everywhere. Restraint is advisable. Of course, for a *Feng Shui* character "restraint" might mean "only one grenade at a time."

Maureen: If feasible, try to show that the star can defend herself hand-to-hand against a thug or two. But once the lead starts flying, Maureen dives behind the dais. She takes careful note of which PCs fight well and tries to enlist one of them as her protector.

The monks arrive: Threats, fighting, gunfire, crowd panic. After the PCs have taken out a few thugs, the three monks of the Guiding Hand leap into the park, over the trees, from three different directions. They land near Maureen, and Chun Chang calls out "Kam Li!"

Not knowing the PCs, the monks decide to protect Maureen by taking her away from here. If they have to kick away a few PCs to get at her, that's fine; the monks aren't remotely interested in making friends. However, Maureen's screams and spirited resistance surprise them.

Attacks that would kill the monks or Maureen should fail automatically, at least for this scene. The monks use their Natural Order fu shtick to evade bullets.

NEAT THINGS THAT COULD HAPPEN

- A video camera on a tripod makes a good weapon, or two characters could fight acrobatically between the tripod legs.
- Martial artists deliver kicks while balanced on the back of a shaky folding chair. They swing around the tent poles to slam into opponents. A

coordinated group of PCs breaks the six wooden poles that support the tent; one shot later, the canvas falls on everyone beneath.

- Hurled backward by a blow, a thug hits a caged bird under a tree, destroying the cage and freeing the bird. The old woman who owned the bird starts beating the unconscious thug with her umbrella.

ENDING THE FIGHT

Dominated as they are, the thugs never flee. However, Phanom Rung leaves unobserved once he realizes his plan has gone awry. (You can give an alert PC a Perception roll, difficulty 15, to spot the wizard disappearing in a flash of Apportation Sand.)

The Hand monks eventually realize that Maureen isn't Kam Li. At this point, the PCs should save Maureen, but ideally the monks should escape into the narrow, crowded alleys behind the Excelsior Hotel. They can jump like crazy, so this should help them lose pursuit. If the PCs are persistent, increase the difficulties of their Perception rolls to spot the fleeing monks. If nothing else works, have the monks escape into the sewers, or even through an invisible gate into the Netherworld.

If the PCs capture a monk, kiss off the mistaken-identity angle in the next scene and have him tell all: Kam Li, Phanom Rung, the Stone of Roaring Winds, the works. The monk eventually realizes that the PCs are good guys, and he offers to work with them to locate Kam Li and the stone.

As the scene ends, a gentle rain begins to fall on HK.

LARRY THE RED HERRING

Hmmm. Maureen's manager, Larry Kwan, set up the publicity event in Victoria Park, and bad guys attacked. Larry has also set up a dinner at Jumbo Floating Restaurant in the next scene, and darn if the bad guys don't attack there too! Hmmm.

The PCs may mistakenly suspect Larry is behind all this carnage. Should you encourage them? That depends on the nature of your players. If they're headstrong and violent—in other words, typical *Feng Shui* types—try to clear Larry's name early on, before they toast him and anger Maureen. One of the brainwashed thugs in Victoria Park could say, "Never seen that guy before." A PC's Divination power, Threat Evaluator, or other gimcrack could identify Larry as a harmless nebbish.

But if your players are the careful investigative sort (boy, are they off this game's demographic curve), you can implicate Larry with gleeful abandon through the first two scenes. One more ingredient in the stew, right? Once the PCs meet Kam Li, they'll quickly realize Larry is in the clear.

INTERIM SCENES

During or after a trip to the nearest hospital for repairs—every second scene in a *Feng Shui* adventure usually takes place at a hospital—the PCs see TV bulletins about the promotional event and resulting battle. Maureen, in costume, figures prominently in the reports. The bulletins alternate with updates on Typhoon Jason, which has picked up speed and is expected to hit the mainland some time tomorrow.

Maureen is genuinely grateful to the PCs, and she may show romantic interest in an unattached male who fought well. But neither she nor Larry knows why the thugs attacked, or anything about the monks, or the name "Kam Li."

Establish the following plot points before moving on:

- A mysterious magician and several monks apparently want Maureen.
- Someone or something named "Kam Li" is important to the monks.

Interrogating mooks: If any thugs survived the fight, the PCs have difficulty questioning them. A character with any Magic schtick recognizes that the thugs are magically controlled. An Influence schtick or Intimidation skill roll, difficulty 10, overcomes the enchantment, as does the Healing Chi power. Or the control can wear off on its own.

The mooks have little to offer: "We was minding our own business in Club Suzie Wong in Tsimshatsui. This big mainlander in a weird kimono came over to our table and blew some kind of dust at us. Don't remember much after that, except we was supposed to grab the gal and take her to the airport."

(Phanom Rung wants Kam Li taken to the airport, not to fly her somewhere, but because he remembers that the Stone is buried somewhere in the vicinity.)

Magical investigation: A sorcerer with the Divination schtick can consult the I Ching for a clue. The coins or yarrowstalks offer Hexagram 59: Reunion. "Wind above, water below: Gradual change above the profound water. Rulers meet with their subordinates. Advantage in cooperation, correct persistence, and the company of fellows."

The fourth and fifth lines are moving lines, which offer the additional image of Hexagram 53: Development. "Penetrating change moves the immobile mountain. The enlightened person improves life through good conduct and correct persistence. Marriage brings good fortune."

The first hexagram hints at the scene of the next fight, the Jumbo Floating Restaurant in Aberdeen, and the arrival of Phanom Rung. The second hexagram, indicating future events, foreshadows the coming typhoon and a possible happy ending for Chun Chang and Kam Li. However, the PCs have much work ahead to bring that about.

Where next?: Maureen and Larry Kwan have an exceedingly important dinner date tonight in Aberdeen. They're meeting with Golden Phoenix studio executives about Maureen's next film. She doesn't dare miss the dinner, but she asks the PCs to come along and dine as guards at a table near her—her treat! If she's managed to gain the romantic interest of at least one PC, the decision to come along should be a no-brainer. If this hasn't happened, she can simply hire the PCs.

If they refuse to go, skip Scenes 2 and 3. Phanom Rung kidnaps Maureen offstage; Kam Li finds the PCs and asks their help, then leads them to a confrontation with Rung at the airport in Scene 4. How does Kam Li find them? Stage an encounter on the street where the PCs spot Maureen Wei, looking dazed and battered. It's actually Kam Li, of course. She tells them what she can and enlists their aid.

SCENE 2: JUMBO FLOATING RESTAURANT

That evening, the rain is falling a bit harder. The harbor of Aberdeen, the industrial center on the southern coast of Hong Kong island, is filled with picturesque junks, houseboats, grocery boats, and bullet-nosed, radar-equipped fishing vessels. They're all packed into the typhoon shelter, tight as bullets in a cartridge belt, lashed down in preparation for Jason. People aboard the sampans are praying, lighting joss sticks of incense and shielding them from the rain.

Nothing in Aberdeen draws more tourists than the giant floating restaurants moored beside palatial Aberdeen Marina. Though the water is choppy, free shuttles still run from Shum Wan Ferry Pier out to Jumbo Floating Restaurant and its smaller neighbor, Tai Pak. These are immense three-deck ships longer than a football field. They glitter with lights and Vegas-style glamour, and a covered floating walkway connects them. Maureen's dinner date is on the Jumbo.

Undaunted by the coming storm, many hardy private shuttle guides clamor for the PCs to hire them. For a bribe of HK$50, they can take the PCs to a side entrance not used by the public. However, such precautions are unnecessary, because no bad guys are on board yet. To keep the story moving along, simply ask the players what general precautions they want their characters to take, then cut to the middle of the dinner itself.

THE FOOD OF LOVE

The Jumbo is huge: two thousand seats, high ceilings, and food in quantities that would delight a Roman emperor. The Jumbo is opulent: gold trim everywhere, ornate Chinese filigree, and red velvet seats. And, even in the teeth of an approaching hurricane, the Jumbo is crowded: hordes of Japanese package tourists, lots of upscale white executives (called *lo-fan*), and European and Australian travellers drunk on rice wine, all served by platoons of Chinese and Filipino waiters.

Maureen, Larry, three studio executives (Mr. Pao, Mr. Chin, and Mr. Wo), and the PCs are dining on the top floor, which affords the best view of the lights of Aberdeen. This deck is posh even by Jumbo standards, but it's as crowded as the rest of the restaurant. The central part of this floor is a double-height, window-lined octagonal atrium with an Asian-style chandelier.

The food: The PCs can select from a long menu of Cantonese dishes: the usual dishes you might find in any Chinese restaurant in America, plus thousand-year-old eggs, bird's nest soup, stuffed pigeon, duck feet, and expensive dishes like snake bladder, steamed carp, and ginseng chicken that are reputed to have aphrodisiac qualities.

Two showy orders popular with tourists are the various sizzling rice dishes, served on a super-hot iron skillet, and Drunken Prawns. When you order Drunken Prawns, the waiter brings to your table a covered glass bowl filled with huge live shrimp. He pours a bottle of dark rice wine through a hole in the lid. The prawns thrash around in the wine, more and more violently, until it seems they'll crash out of the bowl. Finally, dead drunk, they pass out, and the waiter drops them one by one, still alive, into a boiling vat of soup stock. They taste great, if you still have an appetite.

Falling in love: Because it's not polite to talk business while eating, the executives make small talk with Larry Kwan. Maureen casts sidelong glances at the PC she's become enamored with. Depending on whether the PCs has shown interest in her, she might eat with a sensuousness that recalls *Tom Jones*. Perhaps she leaves her table briefly to exchange a few pleasantries with the PC; try to build up the attraction on both sides.

At some point near the end of the meal, Maureen excuses herself to go to the ladies' room. If a watchful PC goes with her, that's fine. Her absence sets up the fight and its accompanying mistaken-identity comedy, for Kam Li, Phanom Rung, and the Hand monks arrive within moments after she leaves.

ENTRANCE OF THE BAD GUYS

First the three monks show up—not leaping in a window, not crashing through the wall, but walking in, following a waiter. They're dripping wet with rain. The PCs see that Chun Chang is holding a torn poster with Maureen's image.

The monks followed Maureen here, then debated whether to approach her. They know she isn't Kam Li, but her uncanny resemblance makes them hope she might know of Kam Li's whereabouts. They asked a waiter to bring them to her table, where they intend to question her when she returns from the restroom.

Of course, the PCs may well interfere. Chun Chang, jealous of any male PC who gets to hang around Kam Li's lookalike (ah, love!), is primed to resent interference, but Tzu-Yeh and Ssu-ma Niu are calm and ready to restrain him. The anguished young man casts moony looks at Maureen, who looks away.

Maybe the fight starts now, maybe not. While the nature of the monks' intent remains ambiguous and tension is high, the sorcerer attacks.

RESTAURANT FIGHT

In the center of each large table is a lazy-susan rotating platform like those in many Chinese restaurants. In a blaze of light, Phanom Rung ap pears, standing atop one of those platforms. (Don't roll for initiative yet.) He kicks aside a bowl of roast goose and sets the platform turning. As it turns, he scatters a pouch of glittering silver dust over the diners at this and several nearby tables. The eyes of the diners turn white as the Dust of Enslavement takes effect.

"Kill them!" shouts Rung, pointing at the PCs and the monks. The innocent customers, compelled by the magic that drove thousands of slaves to ceaseless labor on the Cambodian god-kings' massive temple complexes, stand like zombies. As one, the newly-made mooks—men, old women, children—stumble toward the PCs.

Now roll for initiative.

The fight: For each PC there are four diners armed with chopsticks, metal ladles, or broken water glasses. Their magically enhanced Attributes are Body 6, Chi 0, Mind 4, Reflexes 6. They have no relevant skills. Presumably the PCs try to incapacitate rather than kill these innocent dupes.

On his first shot Phanom Rung sprinkles Bewilderment Powder (an Illusion schtick with sight and sound) that makes it appear he's still standing on the table, then jumps down behind it. He throws Enslavement Dust at the monks from there, hoping that his illusion will draw the PCs' fire. After a bullet, missile, or hand-to-hand attack whisks through the immaterial sorcerer, give each PC a Perception check to spot the real sorcerer.

After the heroes see through the illusion, Phanom Rung sprinkles Powdered Wings on his feet and flies elsewhere in the restaurant. He's looking for Maureen, whom he still thinks is Kam Li.

This time, he gets the real item.

KAM LI'S ENTRANCE

While wandering at random in Hong Kong, the confused Kam Li (still under the effect of Rung's magic) looked in a store window and saw herself on television. She also saw Chun Chang, and a single vivid memory rose through the haze: the young monk staring into her eyes. Not remembering who he is or why she's interested, she has nonetheless searched for Chang, and now has found him.

Seeing Rung, Kam Li leaps into the fight scene from a side hallway (coincidentally near the ladies' room). Identify her to the players as Maureen, but mention that she's wearing the film costume she wore this afternoon. If a PC tries to shuffle her away from danger, Kam Li tries to punch the PC; reduce the attack's difficulty because the PC is (presumably) off-guard.

RUNNING MISTAKEN IDENTITY GAGS

Hong Kong movies such as Jackie Chan's *Twin Dragons* have featured characters identical in appearance but widely different in ability. Like twin stories in the West as far back as Twain's *Prince and the Pauper*, these stories contrive frequent excuses to separate one of the twins from his friends, then bring the other twin onto the scene. Hijinks, as they say, ensue. The scripts sustain the comedy over many scenes by making the confused parties unbelievably blind to the obvious.

Roleplayers are much quicker on the uptake, so assume that your group will twig to the mistaken-identity angle quickly. Scene 2 offers one good opportunity for a surprising "twin twist," when Kam Li leaps into the battle against Phanom Rung (see below). Play the surprise for what it's worth, but as soon as the players turn to each other and say "This isn't Maureen," move on.

JUMBO FLOATING RESTAURANT

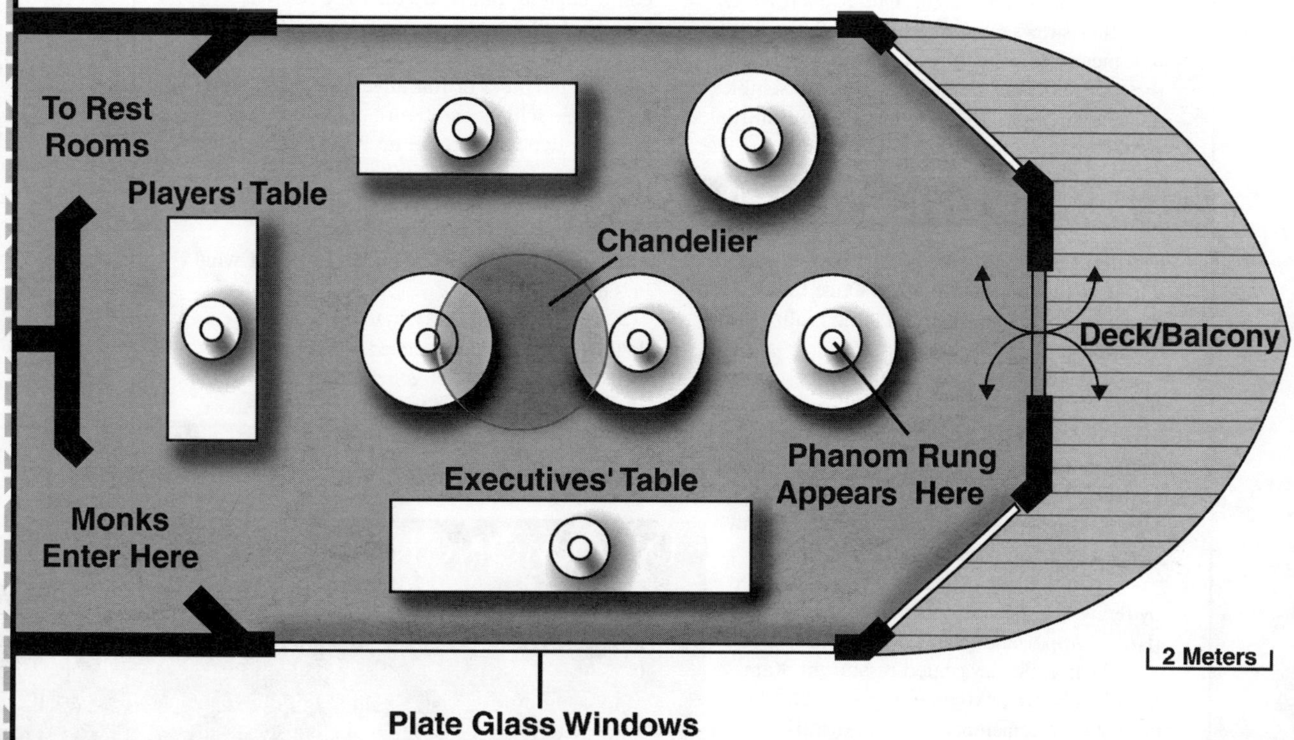

On her next shot, as Chun Chang looks on raptly, the warrior woman leaps onto the table and engages Rung hand to hand. The PCs realize that this isn't Maureen, and they should understand which side she's on.

(Unknown to the heroes, Rung manages to pull his map from Kam Li's sleeve during this exchange of blows. Kam Li doesn't notice.)

By the way, try hard to keep Kam Li alive in this fight.

THE MONKS BECOME GOOD GUYS

Likewise, the three Guiding Hand monks realize which side the PCs are on. Thereafter they fight shoulder to shoulder with the heroes. In a moment between leaping attacks, Ssu-ma Niu takes a moment to apologize to the PCs for any earlier "unpleasantness" between them.

A dramatic choice: If it's feasible, try to arrange for Phanom Rung to take control of at least one of the two older monks, Tzu-Yeh and Ssu-ma Niu. Then Rung orders the controlled monk to attack Kam Li. Chun Chang is standing right between the two, and has a moment to decide where his loyalties lie.

If a PC happens to knock out anyone involved and remove Chang's need to decide, Chang becomes better disposed toward that PC for the rest of the adventure. Otherwise, Chang breaks discipline and attacks the elder monk with a well-placed kick. Kam Li spends a shot just looking at Chang in wonder.

NEAT THINGS THAT COULD HAPPEN

- No doubt you've already realized that a bowl full of cavorting Drunken Prawns makes a weapon unique in the brief but colorful annals of *Feng Shui*. It does no damage, but the target, who is spooked big-time, loses one shot while picking off the wriggling prawns.
- Combatants jump from chair to tabletop to dish-cart, scattering food, dishes, and cutlery as they go. They break the bases off wine glasses and impale enemies with the broken stems.
- Sizzling rice skillets do Damage of 8.
- Each wall of the Jumbo Floating Restaurant is lined with big plate glass windows. People get thrown through those windows out into the harbor (Damage 15). Though solidly built, the

decks are hardly unbreakable; someone crashes through the floor onto a dining table below (Damage 9).

- Likewise, the ceiling is thinly built. The fight could easily move up to the roof. Remember, it's raining hard. At the roof's edge stand two huge neon signs. One reads JUMBO; the other shows two large Chinese characters that mean the same thing. Spikes curve up from the roof's corners, because the decor resembles a Chinese temple. The summit of the restaurant is 60 feet above the water.

ENDING THE FIGHT

This fight is meant to bring Kam Li on the scene and turn the monks into allies. Once these things happen, have Phanom Rung realize he's outnumbered and fly away.

If possible, try to have Rung come face-to-face with Maureen as he goes. The sorcerer gasps in fright and shouts "Scales of the Sky Fish!" With this, he hits her with a Blast powder, a silvery dust that has a nasty Transformation effect: Half of Maureen's face turns to a scaly silver, like a fish's scales.

Then the magician flies away. If pursued by flying PCs, he vanishes in a cold white flare of Apportation Sand.

Back in the devastated restaurant, Kam Li suddenly says, "My map is gone." But she cannot even remember why this disturbs her.

INTERIM SCENES

After the obligatory trip to the nearest emergency ward, the PCs can learn most of the backstory.

Talking to the monks: Ssu-ma Niu gives most of the explanations, with acerbic interruptions from Tzu-Yeh. Chang stares moonily at Kam Li, and Li darts occasional fascinated looks back at him. The PCs learn these plot points:

- The sorcerer, Phanom Rung, seeks a powerful item called the Stone of Roaring Winds, which even now is drawing a typhoon toward Hong Kong.
- Back in 1850 Rung buried the Stone somewhere in the wilderness outside Hong Kong. If he gets it now, he can use its power to wipe out the city.
- Kam Li pursued Rung to this time, but evidently she fell prey to his foul magic, for she was not formerly so scatterbrained.
- Now Phanom Rung has retrieved his map, and so the only way the heroes have to track him requires them to cure Kam Li. Perhaps she remembers where the Stone was buried.

If pressed, the elder monks also explain their younger fellow's "unfortunate distraction" involving Kam Li.

Talking to Kam Li and Maureen: Neither can explain why they look exactly alike. Kam Li can't explain much of anything, being confused, and Maureen's dialogue consists mainly of, "I have to change my face back or my career is over, do you hear, *over!*"

For purposes of this adventure, a PC with any Magic schtick can figure out what's wrong with the two women, but no PC can cure either Kam Li or Maureen. Maureen does know who might be able to cure them: an old geomancer she knew while growing up in Mongkok—"a funny old fellow named Chu Po. I wonder what he's doing now?"

The PCs might also know someone who can do the magical healing needed. If they use one of their contacts instead of going to Chu Po, it won't derail the plot; just skip the next scene and move on. But use Chu Po if possible.

INTO MONGKOK

The best way to locate Chu Po is to ask around at one of Mongkok's numerous tent markets. These labyrinths of fabric and greed spring up each night in empty parking lots. Tonight business is lousy because of the rain. Each proprietor tries to lure customers by making a castanet-like clacking on the beads of his small abacus.

Here in the tent market PCs see sights like these:

- Open-air bakeries sell Chinese custard tarts, and tent stalls cook most of the dishes on the menu of Jumbo Floating Restaurant, including Drunken Prawns. Cooks draw out fresh noodle dough; it's a magical sight, as cables of whirling dough turn suddenly into sheaves of ribbon-like noodles.
- Fat women sell fresh food from shallow wicker baskets: red chilis, wind-dried sausages, white cabbage, ten varieties of bananas, and live geese.
- PCs can buy bootleg cassettes, CDs, and CD-ROMs, as well as locks, socks, and Buddha medallions.
- On the sidewalks, guys sit at typewriters perched on card tables; they're selling false International Student ID cards. At other tables, young men are hand-painting beautiful flowers on cheap disposable cigarette lighters (an occupation that closely parallels the design of roleplaying adventures).
- As the heroes walk by open doorways, they see children in unfurnished hovels, surrounded by towering mounds of bright plastic toy parts. Whole families spend most of each day assembling toys for sale in the tourist districts.
- The PCs are told to ask directions at Fong's Good Health Establishment, a small place selling traditional Chinese medicines. Glass display cases and big glass jars lining the walls offer bear gall bladders, kudzu root, gingko, hairy-legged beetles, powdered toadstools, fungus, tree bark, and that Hong Kong cureall, Tiger Balm. The young man behind the counter, Ernie Fong (son of the owner, Fong Yu-Wan), directs the PCs to Chu Po. "Go to Building #33 and follow the smell of gunpowder," Ernie says, smiling.

SCENE 3: CHU PO RADIANT FLOWERS LTD.

Traffic is light in the Cross Harbour Tunnel to Kowloon, because most of Hong Kong is gradually pulling into its shell to wait out Typhoon Jason. Depending on when the PCs head to Kowloon, it may be only hours or most of a day away.

Rain falls hard in Mongkok, making the housing projects look even more ominous than usual. Looming, brutalist, gargantuan, monolithic: The Tsz Wan Shan projects consist of 33 identical atrocities of the Ministry-of-Love design school, holding 80,000 people on a patch of land about the size of two shopping malls. Dozens of ten-foot bamboo poles protrude from the side of each building; in sunshine, residents hang out their washing on these poles, but not in the rain.

Near Nathan Road where it crosses Soy Street, Maureen leads the PCs through this rat's nest as smoothly as though she'd never moved away. But she shudders at every step, and she hugs her chosen PC to her as she walks. (She and Kam Li wear high-collared raincoats to pass incognito among her fans.)

MEETING CHU PO

Getting directions from merchants, the heroes eventually wend their way to Building #33. Down a flight of concrete stairs, they find a door marked CHU PO RADIANT FLOWERS LTD.—ABSOLUTELY NO SMOKING! The whole area smells strongly of gunpowder.

At the door as the PCs arrive, two mooks in expensive black suits are intimidating an old gentleman in a threadbare gray sweater and wrinkled corduroy slacks. "A thousand bucks by tomorrow night or we're gonna light a match, Chu," says one.

"I'm still waiting payment!" the old man, Chu Po, says defiantly. "Customers pay late, what can I do?"

The other mook slaps Chu. If the PCs don't interfere, the two mooks (Triad enforcers) saunter off, casting sidelong glances of suspicion at the heroes. Chu Po screams imprecations behind them, and they turn and give him a threatening look.

This happens if the PCs do nothing, that is. The heroes can chase off the mooks or destroy them on the spot; either way, this sets up a confrontation with the Triad gang later in this scene. If a well-heeled hero pays Chu's HK$1,000 debt, the mooks take it with a smug smile—but Chu, infuriated, pulls a banana from his pocket, throws it at the hoods, and curses them and their next seven generations of offspring. This, too, provokes the fight later on.

CHU PO

Technically, Chu Po can be explained. His innate gift for magical healing manifested in puberty, but he kept it secret. The Ascended recruited him during World War II as a low-level agent; he accidentally learned a lot about the secret war, realized it meant his doom, and faked his own death in battle. He reappeared in postwar Hong Kong as Chu Po and went into a quasi-legal business. Blah blah blah.

Chu Po
Sample Dialogue: "Try smoking in here and you'll finish the smoke on the Moon, monkeyboy!"
Attributes: Body 4 (Toughness 7), Chi 2 (Magic 8), Mind 4, Reflexes 4
Skills: Deceit 6, Gambling 6, Info/Geomancy 12, Info/The Most Unlikely Things 10, Medicine (magical) 8
Weapons: punch (5), kick (6), aluminum baseball bat (7)

But really, Chu Po works much better if the players never learn anything about him. He's an enigmatic combination of amazingly-esoteric knowledge and mundane sleaze, like Gandalf the Grey combined with Morrie Amsterdam. Chu runs a sweatshop, but he helps the PCs; he can do magic, but he gives in to the Triads; he's a true neutral. This may mean only that both sides fire at him, but if the players come to trust him, Chu can be an intriguing, eccentric information source in future adventures.

RADIANT FLOWERS, LTD.

If Chu Po sees the disfigured Maureen, or if the PCs indicate that they aren't Triad mooks who want to blow up his business, the feisty old gentleman leads them (after insisting that they extinguish all smoking materials) back into his workplace: a basement refitted as a fireworks factory.

What it looks like: The basement, for reasons known only to the architects, is cylindrical; the concrete walls curve up to merge into the curving ceiling. Many ancient advertising posters peeling off the walls depict huge Chinese characters with English subtitles: "LEMONIN" CURE ALL KINDS OF PAIN—HO

CHAI MEDICINE CO HONG KONG. The peeling paper-lined cylinder and gunpowder smell may make imaginative PCs think they've stepped into a giant firecracker.

At least the floor is flat. Here, at long rows of folding cafeteria tables, dozens of women and children in gray sweatsuits sit on adjustable stools. They wear stained surgical masks and latex gloves as they roll up firecrackers, M-80s, Roman candles, and rockets with six-inch shells. In the aisles between tables stand open 55-gallon drums of gunpowder, arsenic salts, strontium nitrate, potassium perchlorate, and other incredibly toxic stuff. (These chemicals are ground in China—by donkey power.) Along one wall the women have dumped purses, duffel bags, and wicker baskets in a large pile.

Lining the walls are stacks of crates labelled in Chinese and English with the names of the fireworks inside. Though Japanese fireworks have poetic names like Silver Flower in Night, Chinese and Hong Kong nomenclature goes in for straight description: Yellow Flash with Blue Sparkles, Gold Starburst. Every third English word is misspelled.

Chu explains: "This shipment is for India," says Chu. "The Divali festival in November. Those Triad scumbags take forever to deliver the supplies, but still expect me to keep up the payments every week! But what can you do? They control the whole business."

But for Chu, and for this adventure, complaints about the Triads are a side issue. He leads Maureen, or anyone showing evidence of magical wounds, to the back of the basement, where he has a desk behind a folding screen. On the wall hang a small calendar and a soiled poster of Sylvester Stallone as Rambo.

In this office the PCs can tell Chu whatever they want to say and get him to heal them. If they mention the Stone of Roaring Winds, his eyes go wide. Chu can tell them the stone's history (see "Backstory" at the start of this adventure) and convey important plot points the PCs didn't get from the monks.

Chu also knows something about Phanom Rung:

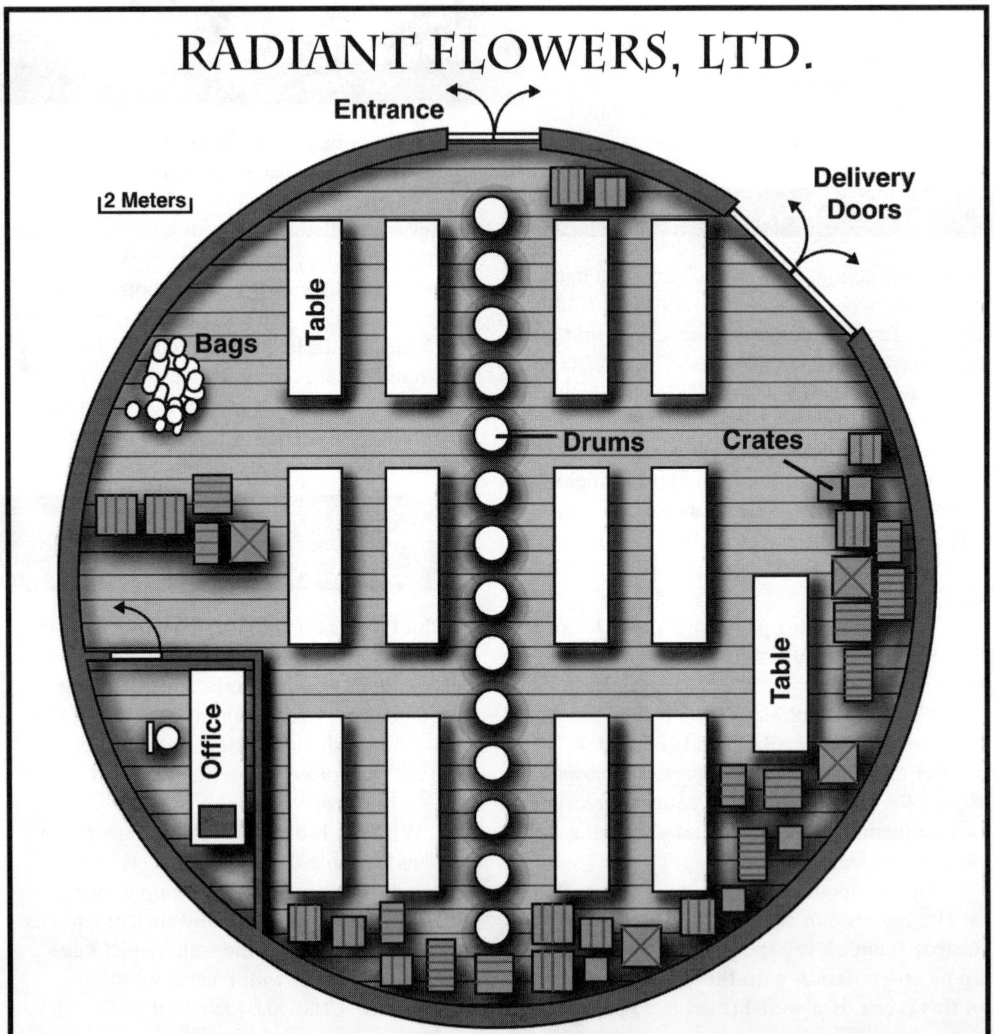

- "That guy must be about a thousand years old. He's a complete jerk, but he knows his stuff. Don't try opening those pouches he uses, or they'll zap you."
- "Rung got on the Hand's bad side, or vice versa, when those monks turned the chi flow way down. I guess he wants to wipe out the Hand's feng shui sites with hurricanes. If it works on Hong Kong, he could pull the same trick on other places too —burying the Stone, jumping forward in time, bringing it back... "
- "Where did I learn all this? In the war. Which war? You ask lots of questions, monkey-boy. Do you want me to heal you folks or not?"

FIREWORKS FIGHT

While Chu prepares his healing ritual, a lot of no-good Triad thugs amble into the factory. The doorway encounter earlier prompted the whole gang to move in. Maybe the thugs believe the PCs are cops, or maybe they don't want Chu to start thinking he can get away with anything. Maybe it doesn't matter.

There are three thugs for each character, including the monks, Maureen, and whoever else is helping the PCs (but not including Chu, who won't help either side). The thugs make some preliminary threats and slap the women around. They don't knock over the drums, and they definitely don't draw guns.

d Thugs
ole Dialogue: "We warned you, old man. Now it's time for a little n in respect."
butes: Body 6, Chi 0, Mind 4, Reflexes 6
s: Guns 10, Martial Arts 9
pons: punch (7), kick (8), club (13), revolver (9/2/6)

If everyone, including the PCs, servilely apologizes for any earlier offense and sincerely swears never to do it again, the thugs might actually leave. (Right. And if the Moon fell from the sky, it would crush the building.) Otherwise, they attack.

When the PCs start to fight, give Chu a moment to shout frantically, "No guns!" Then let the mayhem begin. Try hard to keep Chu and Kam Li alive, but at this point anyone else can die.

NEAT THINGS THAT COULD HAPPEN

- Remember all those drums of chemicals? That stuff is *so* flammable that—well, it's used in fireworks. The thugs never use guns in the factory. As soon as a PC fires a shot, all the GMCs and thugs freeze in terror for a moment. Roll lots of dice, but don't let the first shot blow up the place. Make sure the players understand that gunfire in here would be *stupid.* (This goes for other fire, too, including magical fire.) After that warning, let the pieces fall where they may.
- Gunpowder in the eyes really hurts.
- If the whole factory goes up, the explosion triggers every car alarm in Kowloon. Building #33 itself remains standing, more's the pity.

ENDING THE FIGHT

The Triad thugs flee when the heroes take out half their numbers, or if the place threatens to blow up. If, for some reason, the thugs win, they leave the heroes bleeding but alive, having taught them a lesson.

If the factory survives, Chu Po can perform the healing ritual there after the battle. Otherwise, the PCs escort him to his tiny, tiny apartment on the 12th floor of Building #33, and he conducts the ritual there for the three or four people who can fit in the place with him. (Chu lives alone, because his wife died years ago.) It won't take long, so badly wounded characters can afford to stagger along before heading to the hospital.

THE SPOOKY PART

Chu begins the ritual by pouring water into his stained teacup. "These injuries are caused by powder, and water washes out powder. Here, stick your finger in the cup." Everyone with a magical injury should stick a finger in the cup; if the battle went badly, it could be a tight fit.

Chu asks everyone to visualize these people as they were before their injuries. (Chun Chang seems to concentrate hard on this.)

After chanting for a short while, Chu says, "Now feel the flow of life from the Earth through your bodies." As he touches the injured characters, PCs with the Fu power Healing Chi or the Fertility Magic schtick can sense Chu's Chi essence flowing into the victims.

Things go wrong: Abruptly Chu weakens and falls. Groaning, he says, "Something wrong—quick, give them your energy!" Can any of the PCs guide Chi energy? If so, the character(s) can heal the injuries with an appropriate power or Magic check, difficulty 16—so long as Chu keeps chanting. If none of the PCs have the appropriate skill, one or more of the monks, preferably Chun (with his elders' permission), can use his Healing Chi power to achieve the same result.

The ritual should succeed, and Maureen's disfigurement should vanish. Struggling up from the floor, Chu Po looks at Maureen and Kam Li suspiciously. "That took twice too much out of me," he says, but he won't explain further. (Don't let on yet, but the ritual went wrong because Maureen is Kam Li's reincarnation, and their identical life patterns created a sort of magical feedback.)

KAM LI'S AWAKENING

At the ritual's conclusion, Maureen's face is healed, as are similar magical injuries. The warrior woman's gaze clears, and she looks around alertly. "At last!" she says. "My thoughts are my own again. My thanks to you all, honored ones." (She's looking right at Chun Chang.)

While wandering the city, she studied Rung's map without comprehending its purpose. She remembers the map perfectly. Chu Po brings out a map of old Hong Kong from around Li's time, together with a modern road map. Kam Li looks them over, then stabs at one map with her right index finger, the other with her left. "He buried the Stone here!"

The PCs look on the old map and see nothing but a patch of wilderness near the Kowloon coast, remote from the village of Hong Kong. They look at the corresponding point on the new map: the northwestern (landward) end of Kai Tak International Airport.

INTERIM SCENES

By this time the PCs have probably set up E-Z Payment Plans at the emergency room. When they get out of the hospital, Typhoon Jason is almost upon Hong Kong. It should hit within less than 12 hours.

The monks and Kam Li are anxious to stop Phanom Rung. "He will certainly dig up the Stone before the storm hits," says Ssu-ma Niu, and Chu Po agrees. If the PCs insist on waiting out the typhoon, assume that Rung also waits, then play out Scene 4 minus the storm.

The PCs might want to recruit Chu Po. He won't go with them ("Do I look that crazy?"), but he gives them his phone number. In an emergency, they can consult with him by cellular phone.

Maureen asks to stay behind, pleading "a headache"; she sounds fearful. Chu Po feels kindly towards his old friend and lets her stay. Assuming the PCs agree, this sets up her surprise appearance in the final scene.

"But how do we find this Stone?": Knowing that it's buried at the airport and actually finding it are two different things.

However, Chu says that those sensitive to magic can detect the Stone's emanations during the height of the storm. These emanations will guide the heroes. "Or you can just look for where Rung is digging," Chu says helpfully.

SCENE 4: KAI TAK AIRPORT

Kai Tak International has a reputation among travellers. Because of Chinese restrictions on HK airspace, jets must rise from and descend into Kai Tak at a steep, heartstopping angle. However, all flights are currently grounded because of the storm.

Kai Tak has just one main runway, called Runway One. Most of its 11,130 feet extends out into Kowloon Bay on land dredged from the sea in 1951, but the terminal and the end of the runway are built on Kowloon's original terrain. Across the field PCs can make out faint outlines of ugly high-rise apartments, fishing boats and cargo ships at anchor, and (south across the bay) the unblinking neon of Wanchai.

You should find this scene easier to describe than the others. In contrast to the exoticism of Hong Kong itself, the airport looks like any Western airport—except that the signs are in more languages. The runway is like any runway: flat concrete with marker lights on each side, and a wide access way running parallel. The water on either side of the airstrip is quite shallow.

The main descriptive challenge here comes not from the scenery but from the weather.

The storm: Yes, the weather has been crummy up to now, but an imminent typhoon truly defines crumminess. Most players have never in their lives seen rain like the rain of a typhoon on the South China Sea.

No normal person dares go outside. Lightning flashes often. Winds are reaching 80 mph, and travel is impossible for anyone but a PC or close associate. The rain falls in sheets, so hard that Driving and Perception checks take a -3 penalty. The difficulty of flying increases by 10.

Standing up to the storm: Attempts to neutralize the typhoon using Weather magic are difficulty 25, and the effect is purely local.

No specific skill, Fu power, arcanowave technology, or other effect lets a character remain in place during a high wind. (Weather magic only cancels the wind.) However, you can allow any character with a Chi score greater than 0 to spend a Chi point to remain in place for one sequence. Characters who lie flat on the ground can also stay there.

For a great battle in a high-speed wind tunnel, check out the end of Jackie Chan's *Armour of God II: Operation Condor.*

GETTING PAST SECURITY

The airport runway is fenced in by ordinary wire fences (called, appropriately, cyclone fences) 12 feet tall and topped with barbed wire.

The airport terminal is still open, though the flights are grounded. Getting a gun past the metal detectors requires trickery, magic, or an Intrusion roll. From inside the terminal, characters can get out onto the runway through many employee access doors, but they'll need a key, or an Intrusion roll (difficulty 5) to avoid triggering an alarm. If the alarm sounds, two security guards show up in less than a minute, but they won't follow the PCs out into the storm.

During the typhoon, no one notices the characters out on the runway—or anyway, no one is crazy enough to go out after them. In clearer weather, a security patrol of three rent-a-cops in a jeep spots the PCs within a few minutes.

TYPHOONS

They're hurricanes in the Western Hemisphere, typhoons in the Eastern. They turn clockwise south of the equator, counterclockwise north of it. Their usual season runs from May to October. They're usually 100 to 200 miles in diameter, though associated winds cover an area twice that wide; sometimes they reach almost 1,000 miles wide. They can move more than 200 miles a day and usually last about nine days.

A storm becomes a hurricane or typhoon when its winds reach 75 mph; on the Beaufort Scale used by meteorologists, these are Force 12 winds. Some hurricanes have wind speeds above 175 mph. In one day a hurricane can produce 16 million kilowatt-hours of energy, the equivalent of 500,000 atomic bombs.

Names of hurricanes or typhoons used to be given ad hoc, but in 1953 the U.S. Weather Service officially started naming hurricanes with female names, alphabetically by order of occurrence (the first of a season might be Ann, the next Barbara, and so on). Since 1979 hurricanes and typhoons have been assigned alphabetic male and female names alternately; the name list is chosen in advance each year. Typhoon Jason is therefore the tenth such storm this season.

Hurricanes are the most destructive catastrophes on Earth. The winds are bad enough, but equally deadly is the storm surge, a wall of water that can demolish everything in its path.

In 1970 a typhoon struck Bangladesh and killed a million people, making it the deadliest disaster of the century.

The best description of a typhoon appears in Joseph Conrad's classic 1902 novella "Typhoon," available at any library or bookstore.

ON RUNWAY ONE

Except during the frequent blazes of lightning, the heroes can see nothing on the rain-lashed runway except its lights. The wind is deafening.

(Clear weather note: If the PCs have waited until after the storm, 747s and DC-10s take off from and land on the runway every 45 seconds or, during combat, whenever the GM wants. Each jet deafens all characters for three shots and ruins spellcasting for one shot.)

Give characters with Magic schticks Perception rolls (difficulty 5) to sense the emanations from the Stone of Roaring Winds. Kam Li also recalls where the Stone is buried. If no one has Magic and Kam Li isn't there, the heroes see movement near one of the runway lights. Either way, they find the Stone's burial site—and, at the same spot, they find Maureen Wei!

Maureen's awakening: She's standing there, dripping and dazed. "Something drew me here," she says. "Strange memories." She looks at Kam Li with strange recognition. "We were so lonely," Maureen tells her twin. "We thought that seeking our own goals meant that we couldn't join someone else." If Maureen has gotten romantically involved with a PC, she adds, "I made that mistake. I made it in your life, and now I've made it again in mine." She stares forlornly at her chosen PC.

Chu Po is here, too. He clued in to Kam Li & Maureen's strange relationship, and brought Maureen here when he realized that they had to confront the truth. How did they get here ahead of the PCs? Chu Po harumphs. "Amazing what you can do when you don't screw around, isn't it?"

The reincarnation backstory and declarations of love can ensue while the PCs are digging up the Stone. If they didn't bring any equipment that can break through concrete, either locate the burial site in the mud next to the runway or have Kam Li slice through the concrete with her sword. If the heroes have nothing to dig with or don't want to dig, go right to the fight below.

After the heroes dig down about four feet, they find the Stone of Roaring Winds.

THE STONE

Four inches long, weighing about two pounds, the artifact is a roughly heart-shaped hunk of rock. It glows dimly with an internal light, and it pulses brightly with each flash of lightning. It tingles lightly to the touch. A character who holds it receives a sudden vision of the

grandeur of a typhoon; for a moment he feels as one with the vast weather system. The character delays acting for one shot unless he succeeds in a Will roll, difficulty 15.

The Stone is destroyed after it takes 25 points of damage.

DEMONIC ENTRANCE

Suddenly a bizarre little demon-thing, a skittering demon (described below), sweeps down from the rainy sky. It spots the Stone and chatters a warning.

Sepulchral laughter echoes from the sky, easily drowning out the storm. From the darkness fall glittering yellow seeds, each the size of an orange pip. They shower down in a circle around the Stone big enough to encompass most of the characters. A voice like thunder from overhead—Phanom Rung's voice:

"Insolent peasants! My Demon Seeds now grow, and you have only seconds to choose! Give me the Stone of Roaring Winds and the brazen warrior woman Kam Li, and I shall spare you!"

At the heroes' feet, the yellow seeds wobble, grow, and sprout arms and legs.

Roll for initiative.

Skittering Demon
Sample Dialogue: "Chik-chuk! Chakka chakka chakka! Yummm."
Attributes: Body 3, Chi 0, Mind 2 (Will 10), Reflexes 12
Skills: Martial Arts 10
Creature Schticks: Damage Immunity (weather-related damage), Flight, Foul Spew (glutinous goo), Rancid Breath (base damage 10)
Weapons: claws (4, bypass armor and Toughness)

SKITTERING DEMONS

These little scoundrels are the size and shape of gibbons, but they have round heads, bulbous eyes, grinning fanged mouths, and sail-like ears. They're olive green, furry, and smell like vinegar. Using skin flaps like those of flying squirrels, skittering demons jump up and sail spinning through the air, frequently bouncing back to earth and pushing off again. They're noisy, obnoxious, and bloodthirsty.

The demons follow Rung's commands. If he's not giving commands, they just try to eat everyone.

The demons' Damage Immunity to "weather-related damage" includes lightning and wind. They're transparent to wind; they fly and maneuver as though the air were calm. However, a gust of wind that drops something on a demon damages it normally.

RUNWAY FIGHT

There are three skittering demon-seeds for each hero (counting the monks, Maureen, and Kam Li). Hits on the Seeds destroy them automatically. Begin a combat sequence; the Seeds transform into demons on shot 12, and the demons are free to act on shot 11. Once transformed, the demons attack first with Glutinous Goo, then claws, and finally Rancid Breath.

If things are going against the heroes, have the typhoon winds weaken the Breath attacks, and have the demons go into a frenzy after drawing first blood; they attack one another in their eagerness to drink from the open wound. Conversely, if the PCs are having an easy time, Rung summons more and nastier demons.

Set-up for heartbreak: Rung's own first action shows his contempt for the "inferior" heroes. Zooming down from overhead, he throws handfuls of wet powder at two different targets: Chun Chang and Kam Li. If either of them is absent, he instead picks Maureen and her PC romantic interest. (If neither of these combinations is possible, skip this part and play out the combat normally.)

As Rung's Dust of Enslavement takes effect on the two victims, the sorcerer almost casually orders them, "Kill each other."

The two victims spend one action staring at each other, blinking in confusion. Then rage overcomes them both, and —unless the PCs interfere—they charge at each other, ready to kill. (If one of the two victims is a PC, you might consider fudging Rung's Enchantment die roll to guarantee success.)

Getting the Stone: Rung's next priority is the Stone. If a hero has it, Rung attacks that hero with Blasts to the exclusion of all else. If the heroes didn't dig up the Stone, Rung spends three actions hitting the runway with Acidic Destruction Powder (Blast). Blowing away huge amounts of concrete and dirt, he soon uncovers the Stone, then (if no one interferes) grabs it and flies away.

However, Rung is vulnerable to taunts and similar disrespect from those he views as underlings. Once he has the Stone, the arrogant sorcerer is willing to take the time to "teach a parting lesson" to the upstarts who mocked him.

If the heroes destroy the Stone, Rung stays around long enough to deal out a few Constricting Heart powders, but then flies away in defeat, to wreak vengeance at some later date.

NEAT THINGS THAT COULD HAPPEN

- Typhoon Jason drops a rowboat on someone.

- Characters use a demon's glutinous goo spew to attach themselves to the runway so they aren't blown away.
- At a dramatic moment, the Stone of Roaring Winds pulses. Lightning strikes, providing a crucial distraction or attack.

ENDING THE FIGHT

If Rung takes more than 25 Wound Points, he turns coward and flees. The demons vanish or fall when Rung dies, gets knocked out, or escapes.

THE HEARTFELT DEPARTURE

This next part could be chancy if your players know anything about hurricanes. The eye of the storm is usually about 14 miles wide, and it's surrounded by raging winds for hundreds of miles around. At the speed Typhoon Jason moves, by rights its eye shouldn't arrive for many hours after the storm hits Hong Kong.

But it would be maximally neat if, as Phanom Rung falls or escapes, a wall of cloud moves over the battle scene. The sky suddenly clears and the air goes dead calm. Towering walls of cloud surround Kowloon, but (depending on the time of day) the sun shines down from a pure blue sky overhead.

Give it a try, but if the players call it unrealistic, forget the eye idea. Either stage this departure scene during the storm, or delay it until after Jason passes.

Exit: The monks and Kam Li now make ready to leave. Set the tone of this scene, triumph or tragedy, based on the battle's outcome. If everyone survived, it's upbeat; if one half of either couple got killed, somber; if one of the couple actually killed the other him- or herself, tragic.

Another note enters as the parties are disposed of. Aim for closure and elegance. Maureen either joins her romantic interest as a continuing character in the campaign, or leaves him with a wistful sigh and resumes her lonely career. The monks are ready to return to 1850. Chang may leave the Temple to marry Kam Li, or rededicate himself to greater efforts while mourning her death. The elder monks have developed a grudging respect for the PCs. They wave as they leap away toward the nearest gate to the Netherworld.

After that, it's time for yet another trip to the nearest hospital.

WRAPPING UP

The typhoon strikes Hong Kong and does some damage. But if the PCs took care of the Stone, the storm suddenly drops in strength. This greatly reduces damage to the city. If the heroes failed, Jason strikes full force—but Hong Kong has endured typhoons before and will again. The typhoon moves inland and breaks up within a day.

FURTHER ADVENTURES

- The plight of Chu Po and Radiant Flowers Ltd. is left unresolved in this story. Does the old man call on the PCs to get his fireworks factory out from under Triad control? The heroes might be interested in improving the women's working conditions. Don't make the Radiant Flowers a feng shui site, however; Chu Po knows enough about the secret war that there's no way he'd put his business on a feng shui site.
- If Rung escapes with the Stone, the PCs go back to 1850 with the Hand monks to prevent his reburying it then.
- Maureen hires the PCs as bodyguards when suspicious accidents befall the actors on the set of her latest kung-fu movie. It turns out that two different factions of the Jade Wheel Society are fighting over this movie. The movie's producer and screenwriter belong to one faction, and have written a movie that makes the leader of the rival faction look bad. (No one but a Pledged viewer would realize this, but then, only a Pledged viewer's opinion is important.) The rival leader is trying to sabotage the movie.

INT. PANEL VAN—AFTERNOON

183

Our heroes are crammed inside the van. Outside, the last rains from Typhoon Jason bury the streets in water.

TOMMY CHO

Wow, those demons were tough!

TWO FISTS

Ha! So the valiant little warrior admits he couldn't take them all on by himself?

TOMMY

No way! You were great, Two Fists!

DIANA SORENSEN

Scratch one ancient frigging sorcerer, too. Hey Tsui, what's on your mind?

TSUI WOO

Oh, nothing really. Just keeping my eyes on the road.

TOMMY

Yah, you were keeping your eyes on that movie star too!

TWO FISTS

Yeah, our boy Woo was wooed! I saw them looks Maureen was giving you.

TSUI

Hey, Maureen's a class act. Don't talk about her like that.

TOMMY

So we kacked two big demons and a bunch of little ones, saved the Prof, ticked off the Jammers, kicked Triad butt, and took on Phanom Rung in a typhoon. I never see this much action in school!

DIANA

Stick around, kid. There's more where this came from.

TOMMY

You know, if we're gonna keep this up we oughta have a name for ourselves. Everyone else in the secret war has one.

TWO FISTS

What, like the Avengers or something?

TSUI

You read too many comic books, Two Fists.

DIANA

Now hold on, the kid has a point. I like this idea.

TOMMY

Yeah! See!

TSUI

So you got any suggestions, tall dark and deadly?

DIANA

Yeah, I was thinking...how about The Dragons?

TSUI

Hmm...you know, I like the sound of that...

As the van drives off into the rain, we see the glowing spirits of MAD DOG MCCROUN and JACK DONOVAN looking after them.

JACK DONOVAN

Good luck, suckers. You're gonna need it.

ROLL CREDITS